Charles Manson Behind Bars:
The Crazy Antics and
Amazing Revelations
Of America's Icon of Evil

By Mark Hewitt and Guillermo "Willie" Mendez

PAGE PUBLISHING, INC.
New York, NY

First originally published by Page Publishing 2013

ISBN 978-1-62838-028-6 (pbk)
ISBN 978-1-62838-029-3 (digital)

Printed in the United States of America

DEDICATION

This book is dedicated to all victims of violent crime, those past, present and future--until we all live in a land without violating one another.

Introduction: I am "Boxcar"

My name is Guillermo E. Mendez. From my earliest memories I have been called, "Willie," by the members of my family. Never "Will," or, "William," always, "Willie."

At about the age of twelve, I acquired the nickname, "Wino," because of my penchant for fine wine. Usually, I drank cheap wine, but I enjoyed a merlot when I could get it. I'm not sure that I consumed very much when I was twelve, but someone saw me with a glass and the name just stuck.

I like to call myself the last member of the Manson family. Though I never met Charles Manson until 2003, and I was well into my life sentence in the California State Prison system, I had the opportunity to be housed next to the cultural icon. We became friends and confidants. I came to love "Charlie." Through our relationship, I learned so much and grew very strong.

Charlie gave me the nickname, "Boxcar," during one of our many cell-to-cell chats while we were both incarcerated at the Corcoran State Penitentiary, in Corcoran, California. My name, "Willie," reminded him of Willie Nelson, the singer who sometimes went by the name of "Boxcar Willie." Charlie called me "Boxcar" and I liked it. Occasionally, he called me, "Boxcar Willie," but usually just "Boxcar." I now wear the name as a badge of honor because I know that he only gave pet names to those he loved and respected.

He once told me that we were both hobos in a boxcar, going through life together. We were there for each other because we cared for each other. In many, many ways, his words were very true. Neither of us had very much and neither of us knew where we were going. Together, we grew as we traveled. We shared. We learned. We loved.

What I am about to tell you came directly to me from my own ears and eyes. I saw the following events unfold before me. I heard the stories and details told to me directly by Charles Manson himself. What you are about to read is a true story.

Willie "Boxcar" Mendez
Pleasant Valley State Prison, CA

Chapter 1
You're Going Where Charles Manson's At

"The Journey of a thousand miles begins with a single step"
Lao-tzu

"You're going where Charles Manson's at," my escorting guard said to me. I didn't recognize this officer, hadn't seen him around, and already I didn't like him. I didn't know how he felt about me, and I didn't care. Was he trying to disrespect me by telling me I belonged in the ranks of a serial killer? The sooner I could get away from this jerk, the better.

Most guards are decent people. They have families and a job to do. In all things, I side with the inmates, but I can empathize with the good prison guards for all the abuse they take. Day after day, they suffer the indignities of disrespect, criticism, even having shit thrown at them. They get five minutes to wash up, and then they're back on the tier to do it all over again. Not all guards are good, though.

It's pretty easy to pick out the ones who are on the job just to bring home a paycheck. They don't care and it shows. The really difficult officers to deal with are the ones who get off on a power trip. This guy was a pure power tripper. When he wasn't barking orders at me, telling me to speed up, he was ignoring me as if I wasn't even there.

Everyone knew that Charles Manson was housed in Building Four. So I would be in the same building as he, would I? Big deal. Nothing surprised me anymore; I've seen it all. I've met notorious criminals and I've beaten up many inmates who thought they were big stuff.

I continued the effort of carefully stepping along, constrained by belly chains and locked to ankle chains that chaffed my legs if I walked too quickly. I pushed a steel kitchen cart that contained all my worldly possessions: several changes of clothes, my radio, some letters I had received from friends and family, and a few loose toiletries. The wheels of the cart kept scraping the wheel housings producing a God-awful screeching sound. I was getting frustrated at the slowness of our pace. The oppressive sun blurred my view of the oak trees and the scorched grass fields. I was eager to be out of the heat of the day.

As we edged closer to the building in which I would be housed, I noticed to my right a fenced-in rectangular area with a table and four chairs cemented in place, a pull-up bar, a black weight bag suspended from a gray pole, and a small patch of flowers in the center of some tilled soil. Upon closer inspection, I realized that the flowers were dead. It was apparent that they had been overwhelmed by the heat until they could function no more. The grass was sunburned to a dull shade of brown. I could see the weight bag radiate heat at it hung motionless and unprotected from the sun. You would have to be a masochist to punch that right now, I mused. I knew I would never get the chance to take swings at this equipment. In my building, I would be lucky to get out of my cell for a couple of showers a week.

I was guided toward the door of the building that had a massive "4" painted on the side of it. There will be no confusion for the SWAT team if it is ever required to assemble and put down a disturbance in this building, I thought. Perhaps the large number signified a previous mishap where guards stormed the wrong building or an inmate had been escorted to the wrong cell. It takes a huge blunder for any large-scale action to occur here. When something does go wrong, the over-reaction can be humorous. It would be funnier if it didn't mean a loss of privileges and many more restrictions on us, the guests of the institution.

As I continued to shuffle, I wondered about the other inmates who would be housed with me. Would they be as big or as dangerous as me? I doubted it. At six feet tall and 230 pounds, I face few people who pose a threat to me by virtue of their size. I have been working out for years so my bulked up arms and solid legs would cause all sane inmates to at least hesitate before attempting an assault on me.

As we reached the door, the keys hanging from the guard's belt stopped jingling. The guard tapped the door with his baton. After a momentary pause, the lock released a clink from inside and the door started to open. "Mendez, P-96079, is going to SHU," my guard relayed to the guards hidden inside the darkness of the building.

"Yes, Mendez, P-96079, is going to 4-A-4-R, section B, cell 28," one of the receiving guards said. I heard dull voices in the distance when I crossed the door jam. For a moment, I could see nothing. Slowly, shapes began to appear before me, and then colors. I soon was able to see the large open room into which I had been ushered. It had the feel of a dungeon as I took in the dampness that smelled like old laundry or dank pools of rain. As my eyes became accustomed to the interior lighting, I noticed the gray floor and walls. There was dirt and dust everywhere.

My guard yelled, "ESCORT." He was required to notify the officers in the building of my arrival to prepare for the transfer of custody. Failure to follow the transfer procedures to the letter could mean suspension, even termination, for the inattentive guard. It is understood by staff and inmate alike that prison transfers are the most dangerous time in a prison's routine. It is easier to surprise a guard, easier to assault a guard, and easier to make an escape during a transfer than at any other time. Suddenly, another door opened leading toward an office-like room, which was actually a hallway for prison guards to observe anyone who was entering and exiting the building. There were a few desks with chairs haphazardly strewn around.

Two guards, one very tall and one just short of average height loomed behind a large window observing our entrance.

My escorting officer said, "This is Mendez. Here is his paperwork and his property." He handed over a clip-board and the cloth sack. He pulled the cart away from me and set it to the side of the hallway. "He's cool." He added to put the other officers at ease. Maybe he was not such a bad officer, I considered.

"He's going to B-section, cell number 28," the tall guard indicated to his partner. He then yelled up to the tower, "Open up B-section, cell 28, one to one." I recognized the lingo from all the California institutions I had visited. It meant that they were going to escort one prisoner to the first floor of B-section.

There are three sections in our building, designated by the first three letters of the alphabet: A, B, and C. All three are classified as security housing units (SHUs), special sections designed to keep particular inmates away from the general population for a variety of reasons. They provide the highest level of security anywhere in the California prison system. Not only are the cells more securely locked with additional safeguards not present in the general population, but the building itself is a veritable fortress with additional armed guards both inside and outside. The most violent criminals and the extreme anti-social personalities all find residence here. A felony infraction and a conviction will get you to a prison; it takes repeated, heinous crimes to get a ticket to this building.

Some regions within the three sections are designated protective housing units (PHUs). These designated areas are for high-profile criminals and those who are in imminent danger from the prison population. These high-security areas within the overly fortified building are home to those who have testified against gang-members, and are therefore subject to retaliation, and high profile convicts who need to protect themselves from anyone who may want to make a name for himself. Sirhan Sirhan, the man convicted of assassinating Robert Kennedy, is a resident of a PHU; as is Juan Corona, the schizophrenic known as, "the machete murderer," who killed twenty-five people; and, the notorious cult leading, serial killer, Charles Manson. High profile criminal cases, where famous people are being tried for serious crimes, always peak the interest of the residents of Building Four. If convicted of felonies, the guilty celebrities almost always end up in a PHU in Building Four of Corcoran State Prison. Had Michael Jackson been convicted of the child-abuse charges level against him, he almost certainly would have been assigned to this building. You can only imagine how closely we followed his trial.

Lyle and Eric Menendez, the infamous brothers who were convicted of murdering their parents for insurance and inheritance proceeds, could have been assigned to PHU units. Instead, they chose to take their chances in a protective custody setting within the general population, called a "sensitive needs yard." As far as I know, they have been free from attacks against their persons. But no security is foolproof.

In 1999, a guard failed to securely lock a door in Building Four's PHU, allowing three inmates from the SHU to enter and assault

Charles Manson and Juan Corona. This was an exception to this normally violence-free area within Building Four. It is nearly impossible to physically harm another inmate when the inmates are rarely able to be in the same room at the same time as another person.

Because the residents of a PHU have contracts on their heads (either implicitly or explicitly), there are two added features of security. Each cell has a separate padlock that will prevent entrance or exit from the cell. It takes longer, therefore, to open and close these cells, but it protects the inmates from unwanted visitors or from attacks during a power outage or gate malfunction. It also enables the prison to lock off an empty cell while a crime is being investigated. The cells also have tubes, similar in size and shape to fire hoses, filled with sand and placed along the floor in front of each cell. These protect inmates from anything that could be slid under the door into the cell, such as a bomb, poison, or a harmful chemical.

The door indicating "B-Section" opened with a loud buzz and a click. I saw the expanse beyond the doorway, a hallway that opened up to a large cavernous area. As I left the entry room, I noted some cages with heavy-gauge steel bars. The cages were too small for cells or for any permanent residence, but too big to be easily moved from one location to another. I wondered what circumstances would require these spaces to be occupied. To one side, I observed a small pile of discarded human hair. Some inmate must have given himself a haircut, I concluded. No, at least two, I corrected myself when I noticed two distinct colors of hair. A sign on the wall declared, "Handcuffs must be used at all times." I shuffled along the tier and took note of the three inmates I passed on my way to my new cell. One inmate nodded at me then looked away. It was either a begrudging, hello, or a muted, welcome to hell.

In the distance, I could hear my cell, number twenty-eight, click and open, controlled by a large guard in the tower. I could see that this guard was carrying a long sniper rifle, nothing I hadn't seen before. I made my way along the tier. Outside of my new cell, I paused to allow my accompanying guard to direct me into the cell. Once I kneeled on the cement block, the guard removed my leg irons and belly chains. He commanded me to remain exactly as I was until he left the cell. He placed my belongings on the bed next to me as a mother would arrange her child's clothing for the next day. Once he was satisfied that everything was in place, he stepped out of my cell.

"Close 28. Two-Eight," he shouted loudly enough for the tower to hear him. With a thud, the door shut behind me. I backed up to the tray slot in the cell's door, slid my arms through the opening, and waited to have my cuffs removed.

"This is a good building," the guard assured me. "Old guards. They'll give you what you got coming. Just be cool."

"I've been doing this a long time, you know. I'll be cool," I responded. I wanted to assure him and the rest of the staff that I would not be a problem. I did not need any more of their attention than was absolutely necessary.

I was given some fresh linen for the bed. I looked around at the place that would be my home for God-knows how long. It was as gray and bleak as my last three cells. I sat on the edge of the cold bed and surveyed my surroundings. My six-foot-by-nine-foot cell was an off-white that looked rather gray: gray walls, gray floor, and long, gray slabs of concrete on either side of the cell that were the beds. My bed had an old, dingy state-issue white mattress with a quarter-inch pin striping down its length. It appeared only thick enough to be barely comfortable. No luxury here, I noted.

I could look out of the windows if I got lonely. There were four of them. The one on the back of the cell was about 5 inches wide and 48 inches high. Dozens of substantial bolts held a two and a-half-inch thick pane of dense Plexiglass in place. Nothing but light would ever pass through that opening. The remaining three windows were opposite the back window, one at the front of the cell and two on the cell door. All were of similar size and shape, held firmly by the solid cinder block walls. If a human wanted to leave this room, he would have to do it through the doorway.

The shiny stainless-steel sink was a welcome visual change from the gray of the walls and floor. So was the stainless steel-toilet. Under the beds, two hollowed out square shapes provided a place for clothing and toiletries. The only other notable fixture in the cell was the one-foot-long tray slot. When unlocked, a steel plate fell outward, away from the cell, exposing an opening large enough that a breakfast or dinner tray could be passed to a faceless inmate without the guard having to open the door. The slot doubled as a handcuff facilitator. Every time I would enter or exit the room, I would back up to the door, extend my arms through the opening, and have cuffs put on or removed. It became a routine that I did, day after day, month after month, without thinking: back up to the door, insert hands, and wait for the application or removal of cuffs. Probably, the guards moved through the routine with the same absence of attention.

I pondered my future as I sat on the bed. Well, it was no worse than my last cell, I thought to myself. I had space to move around so my regimen of exercises, which could take me 90 minutes, would continue. I attempted, and usually succeeded, in cycling through my workout three times per day. I had room to write; therefore, my correspondence would also continue, as would my appeals to the courts. In the same space that I would use to write letters, I would also continue my artwork. I loved to draw and paint. Other inmates frequently commented on the quality and life-likeness of my creations. My situation seemed all right. The important parts of my incarcerated life appeared protected. If I remained free from rules violations and the accompanying write-ups, and the system did not institute some new draconian restrictions, my life would continue pretty much the same as it had during the previous twenty-one years of my confinement. Corcoran was going to be good for me.

Opened in 1988, California State Prison-Corcoran is California's largest prison, located just outside of Corcoran, in Kings County in Northern California. Its capacity for inmates is just over 3,000, but it regularly holds more than 5,000 prisoners at a time. It employs over 1,700 guards and support staff. It is referred to as Corcoran I to distinguish it from Corcoran II, or California Substance Abuse Treatment Facility and State Prison-Corcoran, a newer facility built nearby. Because inmates are always considered residents of the nearest town, the inmates of the two facilities comprise more than half the population of the town of Corcoran.

Corcoran, as it is routinely called, has the reputation of being the toughest correctional facility in the state, possibly the country. There have been more inmate killings at this facility than in any other penitentiary. Recently, investigations were initiated to determine whether the killings have been the result of systemic corruption, the type of criminals housed there, or something else.

The official prison website informs the reader of the following: "The California State Prison (CSP)-Corcoran is committed to ensuring and instilling the public and inmates' families with the confidence that CSP-Corcoran is committed to providing the best medical, mental health, education, vocational and self-help programs for all inmates confined to Corcoran." Because of the size, the overcrowding, and the reputation of the institution, the experiences of many of the inmates housed here would not be described in terms so positive. I knew that I would see violence and death much more frequently than I would see the inside of any classroom.

I prepared to clean my cell, an important routine over which I had complete control. I always found it therapeutic to wipe down my home. It gave me something to do and helped me feel good about myself and my circumstances, as good as an inmate can feel about himself immured in solitary confinement at one of the toughest prisons the golden state could boast.

As I was cleaning, I heard the voice of someone calling me. It was the elderly inmate I had passed on the journey to my cell. I remembered seeing him and thinking, Well, he will be no threat to my safety and me. If only all the inmates here would seem so benign. He was just over five feet tall, and no more than 140 pounds. His yellow, state-issue jumpsuit was creased with wrinkles. The old man reminded me of my own mortality. Is this how I will look when parole is granted to me? Will I look like that while I am still waiting to be released? With the exception of his pasty-white skin, he could easily have passed for my tiny grandfather.

I responded to his call. This man, being no threat, might even help me. You never can tell when you need a friend. In my state, disrupted from my previous cell and alone in a new setting, I could use a few. We began to converse in hushed whispers around the gray, cold, cinderblock wall that separated us.

"You settled?" The man continued.

"I'm cleaning my cell." I replied as I pushed a soapy sock across the floor of my new home.

"Well, I'll give you a holler when you're done," he said.

"Okay," I agreed. Once I had completed my cleaning and had settled down to eat my bag lunch, I heard a tapping. The sound was coming from the entrance of my cell, from the same side that the voice had emanated.

"What's your name?" the voice asked.

"Wino." I shared "Where you from?" I was still chewing my sandwich. The old man told me that he was from Virginia. I responded that I was from Hayward, just outside of San Francisco. He knew where it was. This innocuous exchange seemed innocent enough. It could have been shared by two college students or by a child with some kid new to the neighborhood. This conversation, however, changed my life forever because the old man who addressed me was none other than Charles Manson, one of the most notorious criminals in the world: a serial killer, cult leader, and icon of California in the 1960s.

In 1969, the year I turned four, momentous events were occurring across our country and beyond our world. The baby-boomers were coming of age and throwing off the shackles of their parent's society. Long-haired hippies used that summer to converge on a music festival to dwarf all music festivals: Woodstock in upstate New York. NASA had responded to President Kennedy's challenge to put a man on the moon by successfully sending astronauts aboard Apollo 11, to the moon and back. In northern California, an unidentified serial killer calling himself the Zodiac killed numerous young people in lover's lane locations around the Bay Area, and threatened to kill many more. Richard Nixon, a polemic president who would eventually be forced to resign from office in disgrace, occupied the White House.

It was in this highly charged atmosphere that a housekeeper showing up for work at a large Los Angeles estate found five people butchered in and around the property. Words were written on the walls with the victims' blood. The dead included eight-month pregnant movie star Sharon Tate, the wife of world-renowned movie director Roman Polanski. The very next night, an older couple, who were successful business people, were found in their home, several miles away, similarly stabbed to death. More words in victim blood were scrawled across the walls.

The murders sent Los Angeles into a tizzy. Handguns flew out of gun shops; the wealthy fled to vacation homes or far away cities. The police did not receive a break in the case until a woman arrested on unrelated charges began to talk to her cellmates about the killings. It was soon realized that these killings were perpetrated by a commune-living group that called themselves "the Manson family," led by career criminal Charles Manson. Manson and the family members who participated in the two-night killing spree were convicted in the then-longest trial in California history—the OJ Simpson trial of the era. The death penalty meted out against the killers was commuted to life in prison when California temporarily rescinded the death penalty in 1972. I knew the story, but had never met any of its principles and I never expected to meet them.

When I asked my neighbor to tell me his name, he responded, "Charles Manson."

"Is that right?" I was stunned. Most inmates will give you a nickname on first meeting. We are often too ashamed of ourselves and the mess in which we find ourselves, or we do not want to get too close to anyone. Either way, the names given to us by our parents are not utilized much behind bars. A nickname, a profanity, or simply, "Dude," are the preferred tags for inmates. Apparently, this did not apply to Charles Manson.

"It's a pleasure to meet you," I tried not to sound like a preteen girl with a childhood crush. I was fascinated to have a famous neighbor, but I was not going to fawn over him. He was probably sick of others treating him with false flattery, doing all they could to impress or please him. The other celebrities I had met told me that they were tired of phoniness and wished to be treated like the guy next door. I would be myself, I decided. He could take me or leave me. His choice. I didn't really care who he thought he was.

This was the beginning of our deep and turbulent relationship.

I committed myself to checking the man's forehead on my next trip past his cell. I knew that if this really was Charles Manson, he would have a swastika or scars to prove that a swastika once graced his face. For all I knew, this was some imposter and the whole tier was laughing at my gullibility. Perhaps there were a dozen men who all posed as Charles Manson for the benefit of new arrivals to Building Four. There was going to be no punking of Wino at this facility, I resolved.

Soon enough, I saw the legendary symbol. During my first trip to the shower, I scanned for the swastika on the old man's head. There was a faint ink and white scar outline on the forehead, just above the bridge of the nose that made it perfectly clear that he was the murderer he claimed to be.

Charles would tell me about his life, during our many chats. I would get to know him, from his point of view. Our discussions would proceed without the sensationalized media reports, the biased or fabricated tales, or the focus on the horror and death of crimes committed a long time ago. I would, over time, get to know the real person. He liked to talk and I presented a willing listener. It took many weeks, however, until he felt comfortable sharing his more closely held secrets. I listened, without judgment, and soon he was telling me things he had shared with no one else.

At this point in my life, I already knew about Charles Manson. At least, I thought I did. I remembered hearing the stories about the southern California killings in the 1960s that were linked to hippies. I knew that the events were inspired by the Beatles' song, "Helter Skelter," and that an anticipated race war had played a part. I knew that the band of young people who were accused, and later convicted of the murders of a half dozen people, was led by a cult leader named Charles Manson. I knew that the leader was a musician and that his songs had been recorded by the Beach Boys and some other groups. I knew that the counter-culture singer, Marilyn Manson, took his stage name in part from Charles Manson. I think I even saw parts of the movie, "Helter Skelter," the story of his crimes. He was huge in my mind and in the mind of our society. Talking with him face-to-face, I realized how little I really knew about him. It appeared that I had more questions about him than I had answers.

I would use this opportunity, I decided. Being housed next to the most notorious criminal in California just might open some doors for me. At the same time, I resolved to be wary of this man. No one was going to make a follower out of me. I was not much into religion and I certainly had no intension of being told what to do. Many guards and inmates had tried to manipulate me in the past, some for good, most for bad. None of them had ever had much effect on the decisions I made for myself. My own mother even commented on my stubbornness when I was three years of age. This man would not be a boss to me. I had no intension of revering and following him. I would be cautious with him as I am with everyone in prison. I am no rookie and not easily persuaded. There was no way he would have any influence over me, no matter what he did to a group of young kids forty years ago.

Charles Manson's best days had come and gone, I could tell when I was escorted past his cell. To look at him, you might wonder why Rolling Stone Magazine dubbed him, "the most dangerous man alive." In appearance, he was more an affable grandfather than a physical threat. If he were intentionally blocking a doorway, he would not even slow me down. One swing and he would be stretched out on the floor. A knife probably wouldn't give him any advantage over me, not even an exceedingly large knife.

In his seventies, Charlie is no longer the imposing figure that he once may have been. Gone was the erect posture, the wiry musculature. When I met him, he wore his hair long and shaggy with a long, grey beard to match. This would change as so much about him seemed to change from week to week. Over the next few years, he would braid his beard, trim his beard and hair much shorter, and then cut off all hair from his entire face and head.

As I came to know him in his later years, I learned that despite his age and his graying, Manson's power was anything but gone. Rather than being impotent, he revealed himself to be a person of great inner constitution and determination. His eyes gleamed with a focus that was piercing. His stance always demanded respect and fear: he carried himself with a strong presence, yet remained coiled like a rattlesnake giving the impression that he could strike out at any moment.

I continued to wipe down my new home, hoping to rid it of all the dust, toothpaste and semen stains of its former inhabitants. The cell was in pretty good shape when I first entered, but you can never be sure. Even as I scrubbed, I knew that it would get dusty again and often. There would be spilled food and the unavoidable grime of living so close to the more than 250 men in the building. There were nearly 5,000 inmates in the entire prison complex. Even though no one else would enter my cell, apart from some guards during the unavoidable, periodic shakedowns, the mere proximity of people would necessitate frequent cleanings. I am a neat freak, unlike many other inmates, so I could and would spend hours perfecting the cleanliness of my surroundings.

There was another bang on the wall next to me. I maneuvered over to the front of the cell to see who was making the noise. When I put my face by the cell door, I heard the old man speak again.

"You got a fish line?" He asked me.

"No." I responded.

"Here, I'll give you one. Just a minute." Manson moved away from the front of his cell where he could speak with me, and then I heard him return.

A small wooden stick emerged from the front of his cell. I could see that it had been fabricated entirely out of newsprint. Gently, it nudged the long fire hose filled with sand that guarded the bottom of my cell. Once an end of the hose was pulled away from my cell, just a few inches from where it had been placed, Manson threw a weight over to me. Attached to the weight was a long string that he retained. When I had grasped the weight, he ordered me to pull. Attached to the other end of the string was a collection of food items that slowly made their way into my cell. There were pouches of coffee powder, a package of sugar donuts, and a couple of instant soup mixes.

"Thank you," I said sincerely.

"Don't say, 'thank you,'" Charles insisted. "I only do what a brother is supposed to do."

"Yeah, but I say it out of gratitude and respect." I objected. No inmate was going to have the final word in a conversation with me. It didn't matter if he gave me things or not. He probably had some angle, anyway. Like most people in this world, he likely gave first, and then asked for repayment later. I was ready for this guy. I made a mental note to always be ready with this guy.

At the time of the last count, I boarded up my window. "Boarding up" means to cover the cell window with soap, water and paper so the prison guards cannot complete their count. A guard came to attempt the count. He stopped at my door and I said that I did not have any blankets. I had asked for a rag earlier to clean the cell. I used one of my socks, instead, when no rag became immediately available.

"I just want some blankets and I'm cool." I explained.

The guard told me not to worry, "I'll bring you some blankets before I leave my shift." After forty-five minutes, he came back with two state-issued, wool blankets. I spread out my sheet over the bed. Before climbing onto the mattress, I banged on the wall that separated me from Charles Manson.

The old man responded, "Yeah?"

"Hey, Charles, see you tomorrow," I promised.

He replied, "All right. Good night, Soul!"

I lay on bed for a while just thinking. Here I was settled into my new home. Everything seemed to be going as well as could be expected. In the cell right next to me, not five feet away, was the worst serial killer in California, possibly the world. This should be interesting, I thought.

What? Was there no empty cell available next to Adolph Hitler? I laughed to myself. Will Joseph Stalin be in the cell on my other side?

The darkness closed in around me. How did I end up here? I wondered. Am I really that bad of a person?

Chapter 2
Willie's Journey to Corcoran

"What's past is prologue"
The Tempest, Act II Scene 1, William Shakespeare

I am housed alone in a Security Housing Unit (SHU) because I nearly killed a cellmate at my previous prison. It's not that he was undeserving. He was lucky to get off as easy as he did. As a result of my actions, however, I languish, at least for the foreseeable future, in a solitary cell. The prison administration wants to ensure that what happened to him never occurs to another man.

The cellmate was a child rapist, a predator and a pervert. I have no use for people like him. There is no place on Earth for them, as far as I am concerned. When he and I were first placed together in the same cell, he told me all about his arrest and trial. He assured me that he had no interest in kids, never had, and that he had been falsely accused and imprisoned. He told me that there was a girl who lived near him who constantly attempted to get his attention. When he refused her advances, she got revenge by accusing him of rape. I offered a sympathetic ear, since I know full well that not everyone in the prison system is guilty of the crimes for which they are incarcerated—or any crimes for that matter.

Two months into our cellmate roles, I began to see a different side of my cellie. I noticed that he watched many shows on television that featured adolescent girls. He loved Buffy the Vampire Slayer, among other programming designed for the younger viewer. It became clear to me that he was paying undue attention to preteen girls on the tube, making inappropriate comments and staring intently. I then began to doubt his claims of innocence.

Please understand: I am not against graphic humor or the ribald joke. I can cast my wit as well as the next inmate. I enjoy a good laugh to ease any tension I am experiencing. Not having access to women makes the humor all the more necessary. Naked women and sexual conquests are a major staple of inmate conversations. However, jokes and humor behind bars never include the abuse of innocent children. All of us have daughters, nieces, sisters, and mothers, who we will protect to the death. Any threat to a young child is a threat to all of us. Consequently, child rapists are the most hated group in prison, far beyond rival gang-members, terrorists, and even imprisoned police officers. There might as well be a price on the head of each sex offender that touched children. Most convicts will harm or kill such an inmate, should the opportunity arise. For me, the opportunity presented itself.

One night, as my cellmate staggered around in a drunken fog, my rage erupted. I rushed him and struck him in the chest with my prison-crafted knife, slashing at him with the shank I concealed in my other hand. I flailed at him until I knocked him out. I continued wailing on him for an eternity that was likely less than five minutes.

"I told you motherfucker, not to fuck with me!" I blurted out, drunk and high on some pills I had taken. "Huh? Huh? Huh? Huh? I told you, motherfucker, didn't I, you stupid son of a bitch? Huh? Huh? Huh?"

I dropped his head in the toilet and flushed it. He belonged there, I thought. Piece of shit! The toilet flushed again and again as the water level rose around my victim's head. I was only mildly aware that I was the one causing the flushes. I pinned my cellmate's face deep in the toilet bowl. Knocked out cold, my victim would not know what happened to him until the next morning—if there was a next morning for him. I pushed him away from me in disgust and watched as he crumpled in a heap beside the shit hole.

I dipped my fingers in the pool of blood that was forming around my cellmate, and painted my cheeks with two, six-inch lines of blood. For good measure, I put blood on my forehead. I wiped up some more blood off the floor and gave myself a red sash across my chest from my left shoulder to the right side of my waist. I wanted to parade myself as a victorious warrior, defender of the rights of the victimized child. I was too drunk to think coherently, but it made sense to me at the time. I wanted to make him feel as lowly as the children he abused. I think I succeeded. Unlike him, however, his victims had been innocent minors. I felt pretty good about what I had done; I guessed that others would thank me.

I gathered up my weapons and flushed them down the toilet. I would have to find new razorblade pieces and affix them to plastic handles once the furor of this episode died down. I flushed any other contraband I could locate because I knew that there would be a complete investigation and my cell would be searched from top to bottom.

My next step was to call the guard. It was his job to remove the body and clean up the mess. I didn't want to face up to what I had done, but the cell was covered in blood and there was a body crumpled on the floor. There was no getting out of this one. I turned on my radio and cranked up the volume when I found the song "You're Still a Young Man" by Tower of Power. Bracing myself for the inevitable consequences of my violent actions, I kicked the door to my cell as hard as I could. "Get my cellie out!" I yelled.

The watchman who had looked up at my kicking responded. "Why?"

"Because I killed him." I confessed.

A week prior, I had begun to set my trap. I started to brew some my special blend of prison-made wine. Pruno, as prisoner brewed liquor is called, is as popular as it is plentiful. I had saved up about forty apples, thirty small packets of syrup, and some hot chocolate powder. As part of my preparation, I pulled out my kicker (fermented pulp from a prior batch), and proceeded to create new wine. I knew it would take some time to brew, but if there was one thing I had a lot of, it was time.

Pruno is a crude homemade wine. Though we were a few hours drive from Napa Valley and some of the finest wines in the world, we couldn't enjoy such pleasures. Prisoners are forbidden to possess or consume alcoholic beverages. The prohibition stopped few inmates from drinking, however. Through trial and error over many years of prisoner experimentation, the procedure of crafting prison beverage had been raised to an art form. Any prisoner can now detail all the intricacies of making an alcoholic drink in a cell, but if a convict is caught with hard liquor, punishment is severe and certain.

The most common recipes for pruno require fruit and sugar, whatever fruit and sugar happened to be available. Raisins are popular and usually plentiful. Grapes and apples are also commonly used. Corn syrup and honey can be utilized in place of, or in addition to, refined sugar. The fruit is mixed with water to make a sludge which is carefully placed over some heat source. In a pinch, room temperature will work though the process is much slower. A heating vent or hot water from the sink is preferred for a quicker batch. As the fruit mash ferments, it produces alcohol.

Many prisoners keep a stock of fruit sludge that can be used to start new batches. This stock, called kicker, is hidden away, out of sight of the guard's eyes. It is brought out and a portion of it is added to a new blend of fruit mash and sugar. The kicker hastens the fermentation process by introducing alcohol and useful enzymes. Once depleted of natural sugars, a portion of the mash is preserved to become kicker for a future fermentation.

Sugar is the best ingredient for large quantities of alcohol because it ferments quickly and enables even a small portion of stock to produce gallons of brew. There is an art to adding the correct amount of sugar and ensuring that it is completely converted to alcohol. Too much sugar or too short a fermentation period gives the liquid a sweet taste without enough alcohol. Seasoned veterans in a state penitentiary can be as skilled in the art of beverage making as any brew master at Budweiser or any enologist at an upscale winery.

I smashed the fruit until it was a mushy applesauce. I put this and some kicker into a fresh garbage bag with some scalding water to start anew the fermentation process. After two days, I added the syrups. I concealed the bag under my bed, carefully wrapped in a blanket. In all, I had about two gallons of mixture. I allowed it to ferment another five days, a short amount of time for a prison mixture. I was able to speed up the process by heating the mixture three times a day: I lowered the bag into my toilet and doused it with the hottest water I could produce. The blanket served the dual purpose of hiding the bag from curious prison guards and insulating the mixture to keep it warm while it cooked.

When the short fermentation period was complete, I strained the pulp from the wine. I set aside the new kicker for a repeat process that likely would not happen if my plans were successful. I was so excited looking over my new pruno! Never before had I created it so quickly; never before had I made such a large batch. A warm feeling came over me when I thought about my "party" that night. I am not sure if I was more excited to drink to my heart's content or to serve my cellie a nice, cold dish of revenge. Never would he lie to me again about hurting some poor defenseless girl, and never again would he be able to harm a child without thinking about how he had been paid back by ol' Wino!

The last step, after straining the mixture, was to cool it. This was achieved by lowering it, still inside its bag, into the cold water of my toilet. Knowing that I was doing this under the watchful eyes of the prison guards, and actually getting away with it, was so rewarding. It gave me a high that was better than any sexual experience. I would get years worth of bragging rights once my plans were successfully carried out.

Just after lunch, when I had reasoned that the wine had been sufficiently cooled, I split the bag open and filled my cup for the first sip. The pruno tasted as sweet and citrusy as it smelled, reminding me of some after-dinner wine at a trendy restaurant. It was as good as anything I had previously concocted, despite being very sweet. Given more time, I could have baked off more of the sugar and raised its alcohol content, but I did not want to wait. Today was the day I had scheduled for my party, the day I would exact my revenge.

My cellie was equally eager to taste his first sip. I filled my cup again and offered some to my willing victim. By 11:00 in the evening, we were both fully sauced. I was drunk beyond awareness of many of my actions. My cellie was moving slowly, slurring his speech, and rambling incoherent words. I was rolling around on my bed, constantly changing radio stations as I sought better music than I could find. This angered my cellie. He told me to leave the radio alone: "Stop changing the station. You are making my mind go blew, blew, blew."

I laughed at how foolish this sounded. In my inebriated state, probably anything sounded funny to me. Since it was my radio, and since I had no interest in being told what to do, I continued to search out new stations. Suddenly, he had had enough. He didn't raise his voice, or give any undue attention in my direction. He simply started to pack his belongings. It was a strange way to express rage, I laughed to myself. Instead of yelling at me or making threats, he pretended I did not exist.

He stepped over to his locker and pulled out some shirts and tossed them by the cell door. He returned to his locker to retrieve letters, items of hygiene, and other miscellaneous belongings. These he also dumped on the ever-growing pile in front of the door. Maybe somewhere in his drunken stupor, it made sense. I found it comical. Where he was hoping to go? I had no idea. I knew no prison guard would aid his travel plans. He was in jail, for God sakes!

This was the time I decided to set my plan in motion. With his attention directed elsewhere, I carefully slid my prison-made knife out of my mattress, the best hiding spot in a prison cell. In my hand, I gazed at tiny pieces of razorblade affixed to a plastic spoon handle. My weapon was small, but quite effective when used with skill. It could easily end a man's life. I collected the edge of my bed sheet and began to wrap it around my wrist. If my flimsy knife slipped as I wielded it, I had no intension of either dropping it so he could gain mastery or of mutilating my own hands.

At this point, my cellie was totally unaware of what I was doing, and even more oblivious to the harm I was intending. Perhaps he had had a premonition that prompted him in his quixotic quest to flee the room.

He started to bang on the door. I mocked him: "Kick it harder. The night man will be up here. Just kick it harder." The fool did just that. He kept kicking the door. "Harder," I urged, "and he'll really be up here fast." I was enjoying the mocking. He was too drunk or enraged to notice.

I admit that, at the time, I was verbally and physically abusive by nature, not just to my cellmates, but to anyone who crossed me. I've mellowed some since that day, but at the time, I was a mean son of a bitch. It's all I had ever known. Either you menace and attack like a shark or you get eaten by the sharks around you. I had long ago committed to self-preservation: there was no way I was going to be another person's meal. A true convict stands up for his rights. For me, there is no way another inmate, guard, or any prison official was going to gain the upper hand. I didn't care what "hole" or what Security Housing Unit they had to put me in: I would not submit. I didn't care if they chopped me up into little tiny pieces and placed each piece on the electric chair, I would not bow down to someone else and do things his way. I had always done things my way. That is just who I was and what I was about.

I jumped down from my bunk. "Fuck it, do you want to just get off?" I asked to initiate a fight.

"Yeah," he responded passively and without emotion. He didn't possess enough control of himself to protect himself, let alone engage in a fight with the enraged mountain of muscle that I was that evening.

I covered the nine feet of cell between us in one fluid motion. My knife landed in his chest before he was able to raise his fists. Again and again, I stabbed and cut. The knife slid in my hands and broke repeatedly, but I was always able to retrieve enough of it to continue my violence. I put my full weight behind each thrust. I struck him with my balled up fist several times too. My drunken frenzy would not allow me to stop. I pressed my anger near his heart, at his jaw, and all over his back. Even when the strength had drained from my arms, I slashed out at him a couple times more. Finally, he doubled over unconscious and slumped to his knees.

In the state toilet of my cell, C-yard, Building 12, cell 235 at 11:45 pm, the weak bastard gave in to my strength.

I turned to my radio and changed the station. James Brown was finishing the song "The Big Payback." How appropriate, I laughed to myself. I changed the station when the song was over and yelled for the guard.

Once notified, the first guard, the night watchman I had alerted, turned on the alarm to notify other guards that there was an emergency at hand. Within seconds, a swarm had assembled a few feet away, ready to take me out.

Once tamed with handcuffs, I was led to a holding cell on the tier. One of the guards pressed me inside a portable enclosure which would house me for several hours. It was a kick-proof, heavy-gauge steel cage with one-quarter inch diamond-shaped holes throughout. I was left in handcuffs as the guards attended to my cellie. I watched the flashes of a camera as the investigation commenced. My cellie was carted off on a stretcher, bound for the infirmary. He required numerous stitches and a large quantity of painkillers. I was told that he awoke in a gurney the next morning with no idea where he was or how he had gotten there.

A guard asked me whether I was injured.

"Ha," I answered, "the blood on my Puerto Rican face is his!" I smiled broadly, not entirely from the alcohol.

Another guard exposed four photographs of the scene to preserve evidence for the possibility of some future legal action. Once the pictures were taken, someone wheeled up a bucket of hot bleach water. With what looked like level-4 Hazmat suits, complete with boots and rubber gloves, necessary protection against HIV or any other blood-borne diseases, three guards grudgingly scrubbed at the results of our fighting. Mop full by mop full, my cellie's blood was reunited in the bucket.

Another guard collected my cellie's belongings: his television with Winnie the Pooh and Tigger stickers on it, his clothing which was strewn about the floor, and his scattered collection of toiletries. In a separate bag, he placed all the blood-stained items he could find, destined to be carefully examined as evidence then destroyed. He performed a final sweep exploring for contraband. All he could find were a few empty pruno cups. I had carefully flushed away everything else that was incriminating. Meanwhile, the cleanup crew had completed a second wipe down of my cell. They took rags, dipped them in the hot bleach water and carefully removed every minute detail of blood from between cracks and around uneven surfaces. They meant to return the cell to its pre-fight state.

I watched from the holding cage for about three hours as the guards photographed, gathered up personal effects, and sanitized my cell. Midway through the process, I was taken to the shower to clean up, and issued a fresh set of clothing so my bloodied shirt could be inspected and booked as evidence. When I was finally returned to my cell from the holding cage, I could see that they had carted away all my cellie's belongings and many of mine as well. In my own freshly made bed, I descended into the sleep of a drunk, glad to be alone and back in my cell, though I knew my time there was limited. There would be consequences, I was certain. I didn't know the specifics; however, I did know that the event would follow me like a Bloodhound.

I awoke later than usual to the words of the morning guard. "Fucking Wino. Fucking Wino." Using my nickname in a wholly unfamiliar tone, he was obviously disappointed with my behavior. The smile on his face, however, betrayed his enjoyment of the moment. I returned his smile and turned away. My head throbbed out a hangover in steady beats as he updated me on my cellie's condition. "Yeah, he's alive. I haven't seen him, but I heard that he's fucked up real good!"

I received no extra provisions for breakfast or lunch that day. The guards wanted me to know in no uncertain terms that what I had done was not acceptable to the administrators of the prison. Whatever their feelings for a child rapist, they weren't going to condone my actions.

This was in June of 2003. For the eighteen months I was housed in Mule Creek State Prison, I released a lifetime full of rage on anyone, and everyone, who crossed my path. I must have been one of the worst of the nearly 4,000 inmates at that institution. I was not a nice person to anyone; I stabbed two inmates and assaulted two others with my bare fists. I requested to be transferred to Pelican Bay, in Northern California, on the border with Oregon, or to Corcoran State Prison, just outside of Fresno and to the North of Bakersfield. For the incident with the sex offender, I got my wish with two months left on my SHU term. On September 4 of 2003, I would board a bus bound for Corcoran.

Once settled at Corcoran State Prison, I completed my last two months in the SHU in my new prison home. From there, I was transferred to a separate building, a sort of holding cell area called "the hole" by prisoners for its unpleasantness. The only view available from one of these cells is a bare, white hallway wall. And the hallways were often not lit. I had to endure little or no sensory stimulation from breakfast to dinner. My lunch was provided in a sack at breakfast time so I was deprived of the human contact of receiving a meal at noon. The hole is one of the worst places to be housed, but I knew it was temporary and that made it livable.

I was wakened suddenly and unexpectedly one morning. Having no plans for the day, I had gone back to sleep after downing a breakfast of cold cereal and eggs. A burly guard banged on my door, disrupting a sound and restful sleep. I was perturbed, and groggily asked what he wanted.

"You've got ICC [Institutional Classification Committee]; Get dressed!" He barked. I complained that I had to wash up, brush my teeth, and get a fresh jumpsuit on.

"Give me five minutes," I demanded.

When he returned, I was cuffed up and led along the bare white hallways to the meeting-room area. As I waited for the committee to see me, my rage burned with new intensity. I didn't like surprises, and I had had no time at all to prepare for whatever this gathering represented, neither mentally nor emotionally. I yelled at the committee members when finally placed before them. "Why don't you just kill me like you did back in the early 1990s?" I swore at them, reserving my choicest comments for the women.

Two guards grabbed me out of my chair and led me off to the holding cell, where I was to do another two months of the sensory deprivation I had grown to hate. I had a big chip on my shoulder, the committee had concluded. Also, due to my violent past I would not be trusted with a cellmate.

The "hole" was just a temporary stop, as I suspected. Soon, they would need to place me somewhere more permanent, somewhere away from the general population, somewhere I could be observed, controlled, and restrained from attacking others. Soon, I would be housed alone, in a slightly smaller cell, for the protection of others, next to the world's most notorious serial killer.

Chapter 3
Willie Grows to Adore Charlie

"Nobody has ever measured, not even poets, how much the heart can hold."
Zelda Fitzgerald

I was not star struck when I met the old man. In my travels through the California prison system, I had already met many famous inmates and prison guards. After the first couple of so-called important people, I saw mere men who put on their pants like me: one leg at a time.

I met Eason Ransom, a former football player of the San Francisco 49ers. He worked for my favorite NFL team from 1979 to 1983. Our paths crossed after he was picked up for a DUI in Tracy, California. I would see him again in Solano State Prison, and again much later in San Quentin. In Tracy, I also met one of the Onion Field killers. I was introduced to the Ski Mask Rapist in Santa Clara County jail in San Jose. I have spoken with a Denver Bronco in Centinella State Prison. I saw Rick Stevens of Tower of Power, and a center for the Atlanta Hawks, both in Solano State Prison in Vacaville, California. I made the acquaintance of daughter-killing Juan Salcido in San Quentin. I even brushed shoulders with the notorious brothers, Lyle and Eric Menendez, now serving time in two different facilities for the brutal murders of their parents. Knowing people doesn't always make the time easier, however. Sometimes it's better to distance yourself from the bad influence of others.

I'm an ex-gang associate of La Neustria Familia. Once I had received my lengthy prison sentence for multiple felonies (more than a dozen at last count), I decided to settle back and do my time. The gang held no interest for me any longer. I didn't want to fight someone else's battles behind bars: I had sacrificed enough already—and for what? Because my choices and my gang involvement put me in prison, I decided that it was up to me to do my time and get out of prison. Any gang participation would surely extend my time and burden me with obligations that didn't really excite me. The people about whom I cared in the gang were either dead, incarcerated far away, or on the run. It was time for me to start a new life apart from my former friends.

Because I had left a gang, and was therefore a target of the brothers I left behind, the system segregated me for my own protection. I lacked the defense of a gang, and I had stirred up the wrath of my former bangers, any of whom could come looking for me. I never testified against anyone, as some former gang members do, but I was a marked man just as if I had. My status as a special needs inmate contributed to the opportunity I have had to make a celebrity tour of the golden state prison system.

I also met some celebrities who had become prison guards or other functionaries within the system. Homer Williams, a line-backer for the New York Giants in 1957, was a Parole officer for the California Youth Authority (CYA). I witnessed first hand, the labor of a former New York Yankee who had become a prison guard, and an Oakland Raider, now a prison guard in San Quentin.

I never served any time on death row; however, my frequent moves and my numerous run-ins with the law have enabled me to meet many of the most notorious of California's incarcerated population. Probably, I have had contact with all of the notable criminals, or I have had contact with someone who has had contact with them. Fortunately, I have gathered very few enemies behind bars, opting instead for survival and the dream of eventual parole.

Despite my experiences with other infamous prisoners, I noticed that upon meeting Charlie, and befriending him, that he was no ordinary celebrity behind bars. This celebrated criminal was clearly unique and treated differently from all the others I had met. This was burned into my consciousness when those around me began to treat me like a celebrity. The first instance was when a prison guard, one who had previously ignored me, engaged me in a conversation in the yard one day, "He's got lots of stories don't he?" The pause and the open stare after this comment made it clear to me that he desired some tidbit of information, or even a full story, he had not yet heard. Perhaps he would share it with his family around the dinner table or with his buddies over a beer. Others noticed that I was the one Manson spent much time with, and their estimation of me rose. Apparently, Charlie was not a mere name to be dropped. He was a celebrity's celebrity.

I got to know Charlie through our frequent conversations. We often spoke for three to four hours in the morning. Many nights, we spoke for another two hours after the lights had gone down. We always followed the normal procedures for communicating. We didn't want to disturb or disrespect any other inmates—at least I didn't.

There is an art to communicating on the tier. Some inmates are better at it than others. It usually takes a few months of incarceration to learn the dos and don'ts. Many convicts will stay very quiet for the first weeks as they get their bearings and find their place within the prison hierarchy. Even the simple exercise of conversing with someone in another cell must follow protocol, unless the talker wants to be "disciplined" during his next visit to the exercise yard. After a few weeks, even the slowest inmate will discover to the correct way in which to communicate with others.

If an inmate desires to talk to a person in the next cell, he merely has to call out, but he has to do it in a soft enough voice to not disrupt other conversations. Charlie would regularly ask me to speak up, probably due to a loss of hearing brought on by age. I spoke as loudly as I could without disrespecting other inmates who were engaged in talking. Conversations between neighboring cells happened regularly all over the tier. Because we were housed one inmate to a cell for protection, in Building Four, these types of conversations were frequent and therapeutic.

For long-range conversations, to keep the peace, an inmate would call out his need to share and the cell number to which his words were to be directed. First, he needed to clear the tier of all other conversations

CHARLES MANSON BEHIND BARS

by shouting, "Excuse me on the tier." This is the signal to interrupt all conversation to allow someone to send a long-distance message. The speaker would continue with a cell number. For instance, he might shout, "Cell 27." This would signify that the speaker wanted to converse with a particular inmate, in this case the man in cell number twenty-seven, inviting all other conversations to take a momentary pause. The inmate would then say his piece and wait for the other party to respond. Since it involved the inconveniencing of other prisoners, these long-range conversations usually remained brief. Ones that didn't quickly terminate raised the ire, and sometimes the nastiest of comments, of those waiting to resume their talks. If a recipient could not hear a long-range message or could not hear it clearly, it would be repeated by someone who was celled closer to the intended target. Often Chinese telephone lines were formed, requiring a message to be relayed multiple times. I do not remember any instances of these messages being corrupted, but it had to have happened.

All inmates were expected to cooperate in these relays and follow the set procedures. Those that didn't became marked men. Whether due to the threat of being punished, or a desire to fight back against the prison system, most inmates eagerly participated in the verbal exchanges. At all times, it is a good idea to aid other inmates, since you never knew when you might need their assistance. Those who didn't help knew that they couldn't count on the help of others. Most of the time, everyone worked together. We all liked to help each other and gain an advantage over the system. It made life easier for all. The truly anti-social in prison, the one who would not give assistance to a fellow inmate, lived a harsh, lonely existence.

The long-distance messages concluded when the originating inmate shouted, "Thank you on the tier," allowing all other conversations to continue. The transition from one long-range dialogue to many cell-to-cell conversations usually flowed quite smoothly.

It is a little more complicated to send notes and packages between cells. Inmates over the decades have devised, and perfected, a simple tool, called a "fish line," to aid the delivery of physical items. Every inmate that I ever knew possessed a piece of string or fishing line with a weight on the end of it. When someone was preparing to receive a note, food items, artwork, or contraband, he would grasp the loose end of his own fish line and toss the weight (called a "car") to the other cell. The other inmate would then tie the items to the car and signal that the line was ready to be retrieved. Often bags were affixed to the car to enable items some protection for the journey. For long distance delivery, several relays were often required. Participants were well advised to mark the items so that their bag of chips or box of cookies was not consumed along the journey. My first contact with Charlie included a rather large "welcome basket" of dry soup packets, energy bars, and powdered Kool-Aid. The old man was well known on the tier for his large and unexpected gifts to those he liked, with no expectation of repayment or any other form of indebtedness. Some inmates developed a real proficiency at sending and receiving notes and parcels with their fishing lines: these ones were eager to assist the free flow of goods through the tier systems. At all times of the day, slips of paper and chocolate bars could be seen zipping their way across the floor like purposeful mice scurrying to their next place of shelter.

For a few weeks, I was helping Charlie communicate with Sirhan Sirhan. Because I was closer than he to the cell that housed the man convicted of assassinating Robert Kennedy, I would relay notes from Charlie to him with my fishing line. I became a go between when Sirhan Sirhan would send a note back. Frequently, Charlie received food items such as coffee from him. He would often share these goodies with me. Due to the number of attempts on his life, and his paranoid character, Charlie would rarely eat anything given to him from another inmate. I was grateful to receive these items and prized them. I never knew of any poison attempts on Charlie's life, and I told him that he might be overreacting. He assured me that it was better to be safe than sorry. Because I received a constant flow of food from him, I never tried too hard to convince my friend that he might be acting overly paranoid.

When I exchanged notes with Charlie through the fish line, I usually found a few hairs and some dirt that originated in his cell. This told me that Charlie was not obsessed with cleanliness; his cell must have been pretty gross. In fact, Charlie was not a clean inmate. Often prisoners take great pride it their homes, despite the size and nature of their housing arrangement. This is one area of life that a prisoner can control. Some inmates choose to serve their time with endless washings of the floor, walls, and bars. A pretty good wipe down can usually be done in a matter of minutes; a thorough cleaning will never take more than an hour. With all of the bodies in close proximity, men who had been doing God-knows what, passing goods that had been God-knows where, many inmates worried about germs and the spread of disease.

Charlie never worried about germs, but he did worry about pollutants in the air and in his cell. He had good reason to worry because some guards meant him great harm. I saw a guard try to poison him—and it nearly killed him.

It began when a child molester in cell twenty-one started causing trouble for the guards. He banged on his back window until it broke. He threw food items all over the tier. He smashed an apple and flung the bits out of his cell. He broke packets of mustard and ketchup and scattered their contents. To these, he added mayonnaise packets, Kool-Aid powder, and some syrup. The man may have lost it psychologically, as sometimes happens behind bars, or he may have been gunning for a transfer to another prison or to the hospital. Whatever his intension, the result was a horrible field of destruction. After his tantrum what remained in his cell and across the tier was a sticky, gooey mess.

The next shift of guards was tasked with cleaning up all of the inmate's debris. Two of the guards gathered brooms and mops, and set to work. One of these guards, whom we nicknamed, "Strawberry," truly hated Charlie. He looked for opportunities to annoy him or psychologically harm him. Everyone was aware of his dislike for Charles Manson. Likely, he resented Charlie's notoriety, as some of the guards obviously did.

As part of the cleaning process, Strawberry, so named because his head turned a bright red when he became angry, fetched some powdered soap and sprinkled it throughout the tier. A small amount of soap would have been helpful, at least in the area of the mess. Strawberry's distain for Charlie was evident when the guard threw piles of the soap right in front of Charlie's door even though there was no need for it there. He then had buckets of water brought in to rinse the soap away. Knowing full well that Charlie does not like soap, knowing full well that cleaning chemicals hurt the old man's smoking-damaged lungs, Strawberry purposefully left behind the powder surrounding Charlie's room. Everyone saw it; everyone knew that Strawberry had done it on purpose to harm Charlie.

For weeks, the soap deposited by Strawberry irritated Charlie. The breezes that circulated through the tier blew it around and into his cell; guards and inmates who passed his cell, tracked the powder and accumulated scum across the tier.

I told Charlie, "One day if you or I get a chance to mop the floor, we'll get that soap up. I will try my best, Charlie, to get it up before I leave this place or you leave. That's my word to you, Soul."

Somewhat comforted by my words, he replied, "Okay, Boxcar. I'm gonna keep my word and you do the same too, Soul."

"Charlie, my word is my bond and my bond is my life," I promised.

I received the nickname, "Boxcar," from Charlie during one of our long conversations. The name, "Willie," reminded him of Willie Nelson, the famed country singer who sports the same nickname. As a friendly gesture, Charlie just started referring to me as, "Boxcar." I did not need to ask him where he got the idea. I later came to see that he had great respect for the old singer. Because he had so much admiration for Nelson, in addition to a great deal of jealousy toward his success, I took the nickname as a great compliment. Occasionally, he called me, "Boxcar Willie." I wore the name with great pride because I knew that he gave all the members of the Manson family pet names, either a color or a reference to something endearing.

Manson once instructed me how to position myself to speak with him so that we could share easily and confidentially. I was told to put my face between the sides of the tray slot or by the bottom of the door and turn toward his cell. On numerous occasions, he asked me to put my head between the bars when it was already there, or told me to speak up. On more than one occasion, he told me to place my head in the tray slot even though it was already there. It was evident to me that his hearing was deteriorating. Few people have ever asked me to speak up.

He wanted us to talk in such a way that the guards could not hear us, and other inmates could not interrupt us. With his hearing going, we couldn't speak as softly as he would like, and as he used to be able to do. Still, I never got the impression that anyone heard us. We kept silent when guards wandered by; usually, other inmates were preoccupied or not interested in our conversations.

Sometimes, we talked for hours, long past lights out. Other times, we shared words for a couple of minutes before proceeding to other activities. On three occasions, we were angry with each other enough to break off speaking for a day or more. Whatever these tiffs were about, we were always able to overcome our differences and continue our talking. A few times, it appeared that Charlie really needed to talk.

Charlie went by many different names during the time that I knew him, depending on his mood or upon who was referring to him. He could be called Charlie, Charles, Chuck, Manson, Mac, killer, pimp, hustler, father, Satan, Jesus Christ, convict, soul, love, hater, joker, singer, artist, or doctor. There were other names inmates devised from time to time that probably elude my memory. It seemed that he could gain a new handle with each passing week. Most of these were said in the spirit of respect, even admiration for the man's fame and notoriety. Occasionally, an angry inmate would shout obscenities at him. Some of these names were downright insulting, but I never paid attention to them so I don't now recall any of them, except "killer," and, "baby killer."

Our conversations could last three to four hours at a time. We spent long stretches of time pushed up against that cinder block wall in conversation, since time was something we had in great measure. I found him easy to talk to. He was an older brother or father figure to me. Charlie, in fact, reminded me of my homeboy back in the early 1980s, when I first started running afoul of the law. Because I was new to the incarceration game, this older inmate took me under his wing to coach me. When I returned to jail on a subsequent arrest, he was there again for me. We looked out for each other and protected each other from whatever harm we faced. We were able to share information and provide a front of two to anyone who would pose a threat.

Charlie was much more than this homeboy ever was to me. He protected me without ever raising a finger, and he shared with me as a mother would with her only child. Once others knew that I was part of Charlie's inner circle, they seldom tried to disrespect me again. The only abuse I received was when someone was trying to offend Charlie, to pick a fight or disrespect him.

Charlie shared an insight with me one day. It was apparent to him that I was going to be famous now, famous because of him. We weren't separate people anymore, and I would be known to the world because of my association with him. I felt like a disciple of Jesus when he said that. He invited me to be a living platform for the truth, the truth as he would explain it to me. I eagerly accepted the new role in my life: I would be an ambassador for good, for righteousness, and for Charlie.

I was surprised that I got as emotionally close to Charlie as I did. Repeatedly, he told me that he had been disappointed and abused by people. He told me this directly and he told me stories of his abuse. I gained a great understanding of his loathing of humanity. From early childhood, he was repeatedly beaten or neglected. Who knows how his life would have been different had one caring adult spent some time with him. No one can possibly know how they themselves would react to years of similar abuse while attempting to find his or her way in the world.

I was thankful that Charlie decided to put trust in me, even if he could never trust those around him while he was growing up. After my initial skepticism, I never offered any resistance to him, never doubted him, and never threatened him. I guess he felt very safe with me, safe enough to share some of his darkest experiences, safe enough to let me in and see what he cared for, or dreamed of when he opened his mind to possibilities. He confessed that his repeated abuses taught him an important motto by which he lived: "never lose control and never get close to others." On some emotional level, with me, he violated both parts of this commandment.

Chapter 4
Charlie in Charge

"Nobody Steals My Bandstand."
Charles Manson

By the time I met Charlie, he had spent nearly forty years in prison for commanding his followers to kill, and for being the ring leader of a murderous cult. In 1969 when the crimes occurred, Richard Nixon was president and China was still a society out of the reach of the western world. Had Manson been arrested and tried today for his crimes, he would almost certainly have been charged using the RICO, or organized crime laws. Even under the laws that existed four decades ago when he was arrested, Charlie was in serious trouble. He and his "family" members had been picked up on unrelated charges for stealing cars. On December 1, 1969, in a high-profile press conference, the group was introduced to the public as the counterculture cult responsible for the two-night murder spree, as well as some additional, unrelated, killings. The police wanted to impress upon the people of Los Angeles that they could breathe a sigh of relief. The perpetrators were behind bars and the killing had stopped.

Thanks to a lengthy and well-publicized trial, Charles Manson had become a household name, synonymous with evil incarnate. In our conversations, it was clear to me that Charlie was keenly aware of his notoriety. Some days, he bemoaned it, finding it a tough job to live up to, as people expected him to have god-like powers or wanted to measure themselves against him. Other days, he seemed to relish the infamy that swirled about him, boasting of events that revealed the far reach of his influence on our society.

Charlie bragged to me that he was responsible for creating some of the music made famous by the rock band called, "Guns 'n Roses." According to him, a prison guard in Vacaville named Sergeant Rose really enjoyed Manson's music. The guard happened to be the father of Axil Rose who was at the time building his band in Sacramento. Some of the music and lyrics that Charlie composed were shared with Axil who used them to make millions of dollars. Charlie claimed that some of the music and lyrics were altered slightly, but were still obviously his. Though he was the composer, Manson never received the proper credit due him, or any royalties, for his compositions. This infuriated him to no end. When he discussed his music that was stolen, he was inconsolable.

"They steal my bandstand," he complained, "steal my music and say that it is theirs, take all the fortune and fame, and they couldn't send a dollar to help me, the brother who helped them. Nobody would have cared about their music if I hadn't shown them how to do it!"

He paused for a few seconds, and then began to rant again. "There is a group called, 'the Stone Roses.' Now the Stone Roses and Guns 'n Roses are stealing my bandstand!" Another pause and his words came out rambling. "There was nobody like me with long hair and a guitar who went into the bars in Bakersfield to play. I heard the people mock me, 'look at the bitch playing a guitar. Look at that long-haired bitch.'

"I had to fight all the time with all the rednecks in the bar," Charlie explained, "After I kicked some ass for disrespecting me, here comes a long-haired, bandana-wearing guitar player named Willie Nelson having it easy. Nobody steals my bandstand, nobody!"

By this time, Charlie was really yelling. I began to think that he would have a heart attack for getting so worked up. It started to get quiet on the tier. Charlie calmed down enough to start singing the Beatle's tune, Strawberry Fields Forever: "Let me take you down, 'cuz I'm going to Strawberry Fields." He carried the melody flawlessly. His voice was smooth and even, surprisingly unravished by decades of incarceration.

Down the tier, some crazy inmate who had just moved into an empty cell, number twenty-three, started to sing a twisted song at the top of his voice: "Get you, pa. Fling him in the mud. Hit your bitch. ROCK ON. ROCK ON!" His voice became louder than Charlie's and that set Charlie off again.

"You're juvenile," Charlie screamed. "Why are you stealing my bandstand? This is my bandstand, juvenile. That's juvenile." At this moment, I realized that I needed to calm my old friend down.

Charlie could get very angry from time to time. Who could blame him? Stuck in a cage like an animal, stripped of his rights and his property, and taunted by other inmates, he would explode into threats and cursing. He only did this when he was locked tightly in his cell, secluded from the rest of the prison population, free from the threat of any violence or retaliation. He was full of rage, but he wasn't stupid.

Sometimes, when he got angry, he got quiet. He seemed to be preparing himself or considering his next move. It appeared that his rage was barely under his control, while those around him waited in anticipation for what would happen. He would get noticeably quiet, unusually and eerily silent. It was scary to be caged beside this man while his anger was building up like the steam in a pressure cooker.

Suddenly, without any warning except for the period of quiet that foreshadowed his outburst, he would begin to lash out. He would explode over the recent infraction that got him upset. His fit of rage resembled the viciousness of a pit-bull amplified to the full volume of a stadium sound system.

There was no calming him down, once aroused. As he explained it, "there isn't no 'and,' 'why,' 'how,' 'sorry,' 'maybe,' 'I forgot,' 'I didn't know,' or, 'whatever.'" Excuses and explanations were not part of the equation.

On this day, he yelled at the top of his lungs, "I give no warning shots." It got quiet on the tier. Then he repeated himself, "I give no warning shots." He spoke as though he were a tower guard clutching a sniper's rifle. He imitated the sound of gunfire: "bang, bang, bang, bang," with the volume and staccato cadence of a drill instructor. The tier remained quiet to see what would happen. At least, this was entertaining. At worst, there might be a significant threat for which an inmate needed a warning. Charlie, in these situations, would often voice threats to the immediate target of his wrath. He would tell an inmate what he would do to him. He would tell another inmate what was wrong with him and how he would straighten him out. Invariably, there was an implied or real threat of violence. His confidence, intensity, and hate were always palpable.

Usually, his fits of rage became tirades of words. He could yell anything at anybody: personal insults, threats, and criticisms. Frequently, these would degenerate into disjointed screaming against anything and anyone who had ever violated him. He would begin to use the word "You" in his diatribe. It was not always clear whether he was yelling against the California prison system, against the government, or against society in general.

New inmates frequently tried to join the eruption or argue against it. They soon learned that this was not a good strategy. Charlie would single out these new residents for some particularly creative threats or insults. Soon, the new inmate would realize that he could not out-shout or out-insult the old man. Other prisoners would instruct the fresh faces to quiet down, let Charlie have his speech, and ignore what he said. Those familiar with Charlie knew it was futile to try to interrupt him or stop him.

Like an ignited rocket, Charlie needed to spend his fuel before he could quiet down. Sometimes, it only took a few minutes; a short tirade could appease him at times. Usually, it went longer. The average was probably thirty minutes, but once he shouted for a full two hours. No one and nothing was free from the full brunt of his wrath. It wouldn't have been much quicker for him to address his grievances, one by one, starting with one end of the tier proceeding to the other end. His words addressed each inmate in no particular order, then went on to address all the ills of the California Prison System, its review board and parole boards, before finally lashing out at society as a whole.

If someone has ever recorded one of his outbursts, I was never aware of it. It would be fascinating to possess a recording, even if only to preserve his thoughts for future generations. During the event, however, there is no thought to saving his words, on tape or otherwise. Inmates generally cowered and waited for the storm to pass. Even veteran guards would give Charlie much room so he could cut a wide swath. I saw one guard turn right around, forgetting whatever task he i complete, in order to leave the area while Charlie was yellin that this "leave Charlie alone" strategy was encouraged at the highest levels.

The storm would pass, given enough time. It always did. Now in his 70's, Charlie couldn't sustain that wrath and that intensity indefinitely. Once spent, he would go and lie down or he would begin to busy himself with other things. I learned not to try to talk to him after his expulsions of anger. He was in no mood to talk, and even less willing to listen. He needed quiet time to relax and regain his strength. He would often fall asleep.

Frequently, the next day, an inmate would comment on Charlie's outburst, knowing that the old man was spent, and, therefore, it was safe to do so. The inmate would offer some sarcasm, hoping Charlie wouldn't revisit his anger, or he would make some snide comment about Charlie's words. The only defense the old man was usually able to muster the next day was a dismissive, "Oh, shut up," or, "Mind your own business."

"Charlie, you have a lot of talent," I pointed out to him in an attempt to calm him. "Everyone knows it."

"Boxcar," he started to explain, "Cell 23 used to be my cell. One day when I wasn't getting respect, I set the front of that cell on fire. The flames reached as high as the door. That's my cell!"

"Is that right, Charlie? Is that your old cell that you lit on fire?" I mirrored. I could tell that he was starting to calm down.

"Yes," he affirmed, "in cell 23." Knowing that I would be there for him helped him to relax, I think. I was aware that he had heart problems. He told me about them all the time. He also told me that he didn't like to take his heart medication, or any medication for that matter. I may have saved him from some kind of cardiac event that day. I knew his health wasn't very good. I also knew that he didn't take care of himself exacerbating any health issues he had.

Sometimes, I would hear him cough and cough repeatedly, and then act like it was nothing. I knew it didn't sound good. I would tell him to get some air in his cell, but it never helped to tell him what to do. He always did what he wanted to do, regardless of any advice he would receive from me or anyone else. He kept the bottom of his door covered, as well as the sides of his cell. He would block the air vent. I don't know how he survived in that heat, but he managed, while still complaining that everyone was killing me, poisoning his water and polluting his air.

Occasionally, I would suggest to him that he go out in the yard to get some fresh air and some sun. The guards would urge me to convince Charlie to go outside. They knew I had a good relationship with the old man. Relationship or not, he scarcely listened to what I suggested. Almost always, he would refuse. He would say "That's not a yard. That's all cement. The yard I know has grass, flowers, and trees where I can smoke my Pall Malls." I would agree with him then change the subject. Sometimes, when he got on some rant, I would tell him that I would get back to him after doing something. I invented activities with which to busy myself just to give him a chance to calm down.

At times, he could get extremely angry at the guards. I heard him yell at one, "I'm not P.C. [in protective custody and therefore segregated from the general inmate population]! I'm not P.C.! I didn't ask for P.C.! They put P.C. in me! I'm not P.C.! They put P.C. in me. Not me! Not me!" Charlie raved as the bewildered guard tried to explain to him that some privilege was not available because he was in protective custody. I awoke to his yelling.

"Charlie, you all right?" I said as I shook sleep out of my eyes.

"I'm all right. He just wanted to rattle my cage," Charlie replied.

That morning, we had to get ready for shift change. We knew it would be a difficult day for all of us. The guard we named, "Strawberry," was coming on the tier. No one ever spoke with Strawberry unless he absolutely had to. We all knew that there was bad blood between Strawberry and Charlie. Charlie truly hated the guard and the rest of us understood why. We all witnessed the things the guard did to get Charlie riled up. The last thing we wanted was Charlie angry at us for cooperating with such an imbecile.

After Strawberry made his initial round, Charlie called to me. "Strawberry is the reason that I've lost so many privileges. He went into my cell and searched my pants and found two shives."

"Is that right?" I asked as I listened.

"He could have just flushed them down and warned me not to have stuff like that in my pockets. Yeah, well, he only hurt himself when he did that to me. His wife and kids probably hate him because he is an asshole."

"Yeah," I agreed. "He knew you don't like chemicals and that you have bad lungs, and still that bitch dumps all that soap there and leaves it on the floor. Fuck that motherfucker, Charlie. That's all I got to say. Fuck him: he's a bitch-ass motherfucker."

Charlie replied in a way that told me that I had successfully calmed him down, "Boxcar, shoot me your line so I can show you something." I threw my car over to his cell. "Pull it," he shouted after he had affixed something to it. I slowly pulled and looked at the sheet of paper he had sent me. It was a rules violation report. It explained why Charlie was in segregated status. In painstaking detail, the paper outlined Strawberry's routine search of Charlie's cell and the discovery of two weapons each about four to five inches in length, one being a piece of cyclone fence, the other, a large sewing needle. Both had yarn woven around them.

I asked if I could keep the report. "Sure." He agreed.

"Charlie, will you put your John Hancock on it for me?" I requested.

"Send it back." He commanded sharply.

I put it back on the fish line and invite him to pull. He dutifully signed it and then pounded on the wall. When I had received it back, complete with his signature, I thanked him.

"It ain't nothing, Boxcar."

Strawberry was eventually moved to a different unit. He was given a yard to watch over. Why he was transferred, whether he requested it or whether he was forced into the change, I never knew. I was just very happy to have him go. All of us were tired of his "by-the-book" attitude. Charlie was an old man, a senior citizen: why could Strawberry not just overlook the violation, flush the shives down the toilet and give him a warning? We knew that Strawberry would be an asshole wherever he went, in the prison or anywhere else.

Fortunately for Charlie, the charges relating to the violation were eventually dropped. There were some inaccuracies in the report so it had to be re-issued. Originally, the report stated that Charlie wasn't a mental health inmate and didn't need assistance in understanding the charges. However, even though he was not on medication, he was still considered a "J-Cat." By the time the paperwork was corrected and processed, several months had passed. Because this would have violated Charlie's due process rights, the prison decided to let the issue, and the charges, drop. The administration may also have considered Strawberry's inflexible attitude. This may have been the only time in Charlie's life that the legal system gave him the benefit of the doubt.

Other times in his life, undoubtedly, he was not so fortunate, and may have even been the victim of railroading. For a person with the reputation of Charlie, I would expect no grace and no second chance was given for anything he ever did or was suspected of doing.

One day, I was curious about Charlie journey to Corcoran State prison from Vacaville. "How did you end up coming here from CFA?" I asked.

"They had me sign some papers," Charlie explained, "telling me I was getting out of Vacaville and they brought me here. I was thinking I was gonna get out, but I never did. They lied to me.

"They gave me a job planting grass and flowers when I got here," Charlie continued. "Juan Corona built a garden along the side of Building One and Building Two. We had watermelons, honey dew melons, strawberries, carrots, chilies, and bell peppers of all colors. We even had cilantro tomatoes. The guards took some of our produce home with them."

Charlie was not done talking about his early days in Corcoran. "I used to pass out rubber gloves to the tower guards in all the buildings," he explained, "until this black dude told the guards that I had marijuana. They sent me to Pelican Bay Prison. My heart started giving me trouble there so they brought me back here."

"They never should have sent you there in the first place," I commented. "This is your home. You opened this prison."

"I sure did," Charlie agreed, and then his tone turned melancholy as he recalled his first days in Corcoran. "They told me I was getting out."

Charlie also told me that around the time he arrived, the skinheads sent him a letter with the unusual phrase, "88 is Charlie's Gate." The Skinheads thought Charlie was going to be paroled in 1988. Since "H" is the eighth letter in the alphabet, "88" meant "HH" or "heil Hitler." The Skinheads hoped that upon his release, Manson would send them some money for their cause. When he told me this, I suggested that he might get out in "08" meaning 2008, during the thirty-seventh anniversary of his conviction. Anniversaries always generated more Manson interest. Perhaps that attention could be turned into some sympathy.

His behavior shouldn't keep him in jail, I thought. He was usually cooperative and obedient. The guards treated him favorably for his cooperation. They would give him extra lunches, which he would promptly give to anyone on the tier who might be hungry.

Many people, because of sensationalized media coverage, only know Charlie from the dark video clips on television. They know him for his female followers who shaved their heads and crawled on their knees several blocks to the Los Angeles Courthouse for his trial. However, the girls didn't enact those crazy antics only for the benefit of Charlie. My friend made it very clear to me that what they did, they did to protest all injustice: that done to him, but also all injustice done to anyone.

Charlie told me that during his trial, he was never allowed to have witnesses speak on his behalf. Only the prosecution was allowed to have witnesses speak about him and the Manson family, he explained to me. He wanted me to see him as much more than the media "boogeyman" or the face of evil that he had been made out to be.

I asked him numerous times whether he was Jesus or Satan. My questioning was usually prompted by an unusual statement from Charlie in which he implied that he was one or the other of the two (sometimes even both). He had this way of implying it, without actually saying it, in his stories and in his words. In response to each of my queries, he would always reply, "That's who people say I am." I came to hear that response from Charlie again and again, "That's who people say I am."

I have come to see him as intelligent, creative, and God-only-knows-how patient. He has endured a lot of ridicule for the crimes, the murder of seven people. I never believed that he committed them. Even though he has never denounced the slayings done those two fateful nights, I didn't think that they should be held against him. Refusing to denounce doesn't make him guilty. The law states that he has the right to remain silent.

He has chosen to hold his peace even as society made him the scapegoat of all if its ills: the hippies, the draft dodgers, the public protestors across America, and the Viet Nam war. It's easier to blame him than expect society to take responsibility for its own problems. In fact, Charlie has only been convicted for being the oldest and most influential member of the Manson family. He repeatedly denied ever committing or condoning a murder.

Nevertheless, every year, Manson is convicted all over again in the media. If he were ever retried, he would be found not guilty, and would likely come away with a large settlement for judicial misconduct. I asked him once why he didn't seek to have his case retried. "Even if my case were to be retried," he confided, "I might end up back on death row for some other murder they would pin on me." He told me that he had chosen to live a humble life, living each day to the fullest knowing that his time might be short. Not only was he given a life sentence, but his health was not that great.

He was acutely aware of his physical challenges. On various occasions, he told me about his heart problems, his colon cancer, and his emphysema. In addition to his physical ailments, he was also threatened with death every day from the many inmates who would love to make a name for themselves by "offing" the most notorious convict in America.

Parole did not appear to be a likely possibility to Charlie. He told me that many members of the victim's families sit on, or control, parole boards, which have a major influence on the Board of Prison Term, the committee tasked with the responsibility to decide whether an inmate is paroled or not. These victim advocates see to it that Manson is not granted parole. It would be nice to think that this kind of activity was rare; however, it happens to inmates all the time. I have seen it.

I have a friend who is serving "seven to life." In other words, he has to serve at least seven years of incarceration, but his sentence could continue for his whole, natural life. The actual length depended on what the parole board would decide. No matter how many AA meetings this friend attended, no matter what he did to reform his life, he never made it out. After sixteen years, the Board of Prison Term recommended him for parole. When the governor's office caught wind of the plan, it made sure that he was once again denied parole. That was in 1991. Today, he languishes in prison still.

In the years since the early 1990s, the prison system has steadily taken away prisoner's rights and privileges. Under California Governor Pete Wilson, rehabilitation programs were stripped away from the inmates, sugar was replaced by cancer-causing sugar substitutes, and rules for possessions have been tightened. It seems that politicians would rather build a new prison than a new elementary school in the ghetto. Charlie helped me see this. It is more profitable and politically beneficial to provide money to richer counties and wealthy communities, than to provide funds where they are needed most.

It is better, in some people's estimation, to buy a pair of handcuffs than to purchase a school book for a kindergarten student, a book would ensure that a child will turn out successful. Currently, there are more prisons in California than in any other state. That doesn't even include hospitals, federal prisons, camps, or county lock-ups. When you realize the huge business that the prison system is, and consider the people making money off of it, the job security and profits for investors through state bonds or affiliated companies, it gets kind of scary for the powerless inmate. I have only come to understand this lately. I was never much into politics until Charlie explained to me how so much of our world works. Instead of using its power to gain more power and money, the prison system should be about helping others.

When Charlie and I spoke, our discussion was often about how to help other people. Charlie would say, "Love your brother, help your brother, and help one another." He would also say, "To love your brother is to love yourself. To love yourself is to love your brother." He would even sing this from time to time.

His main objective in teaching others was to get everyone to help one another like it used to be. "Everyone in and out of prison is your brother or your sister," he would tell me. "The true convicts were the ones in the 1960s, 1970s, and 1980s, when inmates were there for those in need. At that time, it didn't matter if you went to a county jail or a federal institution, if you had a need, others would help you. It didn't matter whether the other person was wealthy or couldn't scratch two cents together: whatever you needed would be provided. People helped each other with hygiene items, writing paper, and food. No questions asked."

We do not see this much anymore, we lamented.

Charlie told me, "If we help one another, we make this world a better place to live. How do we say we are for peace in the world when we are trying to sell a rifle that can kill at 300 yards? How do we say we are for better air when we seek huge profits in our oil stocks?" These are subjects I discussed with Charlie. We would go on for hours.

One time, he really made me laugh. He said, "Tell that cowboy he has to stop driving that pick-up truck because it's causing pollution in the air. It's causing birth defects, and the cowboy will say that he needs the truck to drive, feed the cows, and go to the rodeo. He reasons that he won't be around in 50 years so why should he worry. What does he care about the ozone? Or, what the ozone is, anyway?" We would laugh out loud because it is so true--how easy it is for people to be ignorant and selfish, pretending that it does not matter or that problems don't exist. He may have been referring to President George W. Bush, but I suspect he meant any cowboy. Charlie was not much into politics, except to point out the enticing trap of power that exists in every part of our society.

One night at about 10:00 in the evening, I had prepared and consumed a large quantity of pruno and was feeling pretty good. I called to Charlie to ask him some questions. Probably, I did not have the nerve to ask him these questions while I was sober.

"Hey, Soul. You over there?" I inquired while banging on the wall.

"How are you, Boxcar? I could smell the vapors when you broke the wine down," Manson said to me.

"Yeah, I knew you would smell it over there," I continued. "Charlie, there are some questions I'd like to ask you. Do you mind me asking them? They are kind of personal, but I'm sure you won't mind."

"What do you want to know, Soul?" He knew I was drunk from the slurring of my words.

"Charlie, have you ever sucked dick?" I dared to ask.

"Yeah," he replied without elaborating.

"Charlie, have you ever had sex with a man who was, you know, who was behind you?" I think I stumbled over my words from fear and from pruno.

"Yeah, but I didn't like it too much," was his reply.

Charlie answered those questions very calmly, but then snapped at me for my timidity, "Why didn't you just ask me if I was a homosexual instead of beating around the bush and asking about specific acts?"

"I didn't know if I should ask you like that and have you feel offended," I defended myself.

"I said it was all right to ask me some questions, didn't I?" Charlie asked. "Well, then, it's okay to ask. You dig?" Charlie was raising his voice by this time, but I doubted that anyone else could hear him.

"In that case, I have a couple more questions for you, Charlie." The pruno was providing me with great boldness. "What is your favorite flavor of ice-cream and what is your favorite color?" He replied that Vanilla was his favorite flavor of ice-cream; red and black, his two favorite colors.

"Have you ever been to Hayward, Charlie? It's near Oakland." I was feeling talkative so I kept up my questioning.

"No, I don't think so," he told me. "I've been to Oakland."

"Is that right, Charlie?"

"Yes, it is. Now I'm going to get back to what I was doing before you called me over to ask all your crazy questions, all drunk on pulky." He was getting testy, but I did not care. I still wanted to talk.

"I wanted to know your favorite color because that chick from Hollywood, whose letter you gave me, wanted to know." I continued. "I wanted to know your favorite flavor of ice-cream so I could give you my ice-cream next time we have that flavor on the tier.

"Hey, Charlie, guess what?" I was entering dangerous territory and I knew it.

"What?" He replied gruffly.

"I've always wanted to get my dick sucked by someone who had no teeth," I taunted.

"Boxcar," he said more annoyed than angered. "You are drunk. Go lie down and get some sleep."

"Charlie, you got a real, real pretty mouth." I was laughing and feeling very relaxed. I went back to my radio to listen to my oldies station. From time to time, I would call him over if there was a song on that I thought he would enjoy.

I knew he had false teeth. When he took them out, he sounded really old. I would tease him and ask him to take his teeth out so I could hear what a really old man sounds like. He was good natured about my teasing as a mother dog would be with the playfulness of her litter.

I gathered up my courage and finally asked him that night, "Are you gay?" I guessed that I would not dare ask once the alcohol wore off. I was already taunting him playfully and he was not getting upset. What did I have to lose by asking?

"Yes," was his only reply.

I was surprised at his answer, probably more surprised at his candor than his confession. I knew he had been portrayed on television and in movies as a womanizing pimp. He was surrounded by his family that consisted mostly of young women. As I got to know him, I suspected that the aura was more about his power in controlling others than in any sexual magnetism. The women were mere prostitutes to him, people who could make him some money and who were open to his manipulations.

Wow, I thought. I was right. Charlie is gay!

Charlie and I were never sexually involved, but we did have a playful relationship nonetheless. Sometimes, when I was out of my cell, I would wiggle the padlock on his door. I only did this when I knew he was awake so that I didn't disrespect him. Like a tiger in the grass, he would whip his head around to see who was there and whether there was a threat to him. In retrospect, perhaps I was cruel in doing this, but it was so funny to see him jump into action.

He would get me, too, though. He would never let one of my pranks go unanswered. He would ask a guard to cut my shower short so I would be left with soap in my hair when the water stopped prematurely. He would ask a guard to slam my tray slot closed after a meal was delivered, or after I had received a book or my mail. Guards generally would not do that kind of bidding for an inmate. For Charlie, they made an exception. I would get startled or annoyed by the sound of the crashing metal as the guard fulfilled Charlie's request.

I knew that Charlie was behind it, paying me back for my insolence. The actions had Charlie's name written all over them. The guards would not cut my shower short or bang my tray slot unnecessarily. Charlie did these and many other pranks to remind me and everyone else that this was HIS "bandstand." He made sure than no one on the tier would ever steal his "bandstand."

Chapter 5
Charlie's Early Years

*"I cannot think of any need in childhood as strong as the need
for a father's protection."*
Sigmund Freud

As one long day led to another, and we got accustomed to hearing
each other's voices, Charlie and I began to trust one another. When
the interpersonal risk level reached a certain threshold, he began to
share with me some of the childhood experiences that made him the
person he became. I wasn't always sure whether he was telling me the
truth, however. I have always had a tough time accepting at face value
what anyone said. By that time in my life, I had concluded that most
people tell lies most of the time. The truth will get you in trouble. It is
better to shade the truth, or make up stories and facts that are useful.
I know I'm not alone. In jail, a story is as likely to be as phony as a
three dollar bill as it is to be an accurate accounting of events. With
good reason, all people who have done time in prison tend not to trust
others. If you take people at their word, the prison system would have
to be full of innocent, wrongfully convicted, people who just happened
to be in the wrong place at the wrong time, or happened to be on the
receiving end of some police or political vendetta. Charlie, however,

seemed very sincere when he shared with me. He spoke from the heart, and I could tell that it was painful for him to describe his early years. He demanded the truth from me and was never satisfied with partial truths or manufactured facts. In time, I learned to accept as truth the things he told me, and to reciprocate an honest presentation of reality.

Charlie was born in 1934, under the same sign as me: the Scorpio. He arrived in Ohio to an irresponsible, unmarried girl who had just turned 16. Neither Charlie nor his mother ever knew for certain who his father was, though his mom suspected a certain encounter was responsible for him. In Charlie's words, "everyone in town was doing my mother." Much of his first few years were spent at the home of the parent's of Charlie's mother. Charlie's mom was not one to be tied down so the two moved frequently. He acquired a couple of half-sisters later in life.

Charlie had some happy memories of his days in Virginia, one of the many places that he called home. Nothing is left of his childhood residence, he told me. It had been demolished so that a large dam could be erected. "You used to be able to drop in a fishing line and pull out all sorts of fish," he lamented to me. "You could see deer walking in the area. Now, everyone says that it's all gone. The dam is more important because it makes money and fills the rich people's pockets, rich people who don't even live in Virginia. All they want to do is build dams, kill the deer, dry up the creeks, pollute the air, dump chemicals and run all the small people out of town."

His grandfather being a veteran of WWI, Charlie enjoyed playing with the medals, knives, and guns that were stored in a locked box in the attic. He had two uncles that he remembered from his early years: one who died in prison of tuberculosis and another who worked for the railroad. Charlie vividly recalled visits he made with his mother to see his incarcerated uncle. On one occasion, he observed his uncle working at something in the toilet of his cell. At the time, Charlie concluded that the man was attempting to escape. Only years later did he realize that his uncle was washing his clothes in the time-honored tradition of plugging up the cell latrine, putting soap in the toilet bowl, and scrubbing (often followed by a cleaning of the whole cell with the same soapy water). Charlie laughed and laughed when he recalled his early misunderstanding.

In addition to these uncles by blood, Charlie was introduced to many,

many other men, always called, "Uncle John," whom he later concluded were prostitution "Johns." Frequently, Charlie was told to play in the yard, even if it was cold, even if was dark, so that his mother could have time alone in with the current "Uncle John." It was confusing and alienating for young Charlie. The one person who provided any sort of consistency in his life frequently rejected and abandoned him.

The men came and went in Charlie's early life. Some stayed for a few days or even months. Always, they left. Some of them were friendly to the boy; others were hostile and openly resentful of him.

Prostitution was not the only source of income for Charlie's mom. The mother and son family was sometimes supported by her occasional jobs, none very steady or lucrative. It seemed to Charlie that he and his mother were always moving. They lived in numerous states, in countless cities, as she flitted from one job and living location to the next.

Charlie's mom sent him to live with an uncle at one point. She would sometimes leave him with a neighbor or relative and not return for many days, but this was different. The uncle, who may not have even been a relative, agreed to take care of and raise Charlie until his mom got her life in order.

Charlie told me that when he was eight years of age he was forced by this uncle to wear a dress to school. Charlie had come running home because some of the other kids were picking on him because he was the smallest child in his grade. Other children had started to tease him after school. When he ignored them, hoping that the passive response would put an end to the taunting, one large bully approached and hit him in the face. Charlie had run all the way home full of dirt, tears, and fear that the boy would follow him to continue what he had started. Charlie was crying when his uncle found him.

"Charlie, what are you crying for?" the uncle demanded.

"A kid hit me up so I ran home," Charlie replied between sobs.

"You did what, boy?" The uncle was not pleased with the cowardice. He slapped Charlie on the side of the head so hard that the young boy felt a tingling in his ear and could not hear out of that ear for days.

The next morning, the uncle insisted that Charlie put on a red dress and attend school dressed as a girl. "After school," the man instructed, "I want you to find that bully and hit him as hard as you can. Don't come home until the guy is bleeding or on the ground."

Reluctantly, Charlie followed the instructions. He was ridiculed for his attire and was the brunt of much teasing. Once school had been let out, as his uncle had instructed him, he sought out the bully and punched him in the face. The bully was felled by the smallest kid in his grade. The fighting didn't end, however. Charlie straddled the larger boy and began hitting him again and again. Another student ran to summon the teacher who promptly arrived to pull Charlie off of the bully. The teacher sent them to their respective homes with a stern warning. Charlie, who had been utterly humiliated by being forced to wear the dress, was now empowered to take matters into his own hands when necessary.

The bully didn't mess with him after that. "I fought lots of other kids that year," he confessed. "I became a holy terror." Never again did he fail to stand up to a bully.

Charlie recounted for me another influential childhood event. His mom had been working in a bar while they were living above it in a single room, furnished with only a simple bed and dresser. About the age of nine, Charlie's already chaotic life was further disturbed by a fight in the bar. A man was making passes at Charlie's mom, demanding sex or some drunken fondling. To repel the man, his mother picked up a liquor bottle and broke it over his head. Fearing the repercussions, especially from other gang members, since this man was a "Beanie Brother" with ties to the West Virginia prison system, Charlie's mom decided to flee the area. The man was bad news and she knew it.

Charlie's mother rushed upstairs, woke Charlie, and ordered him to help her gather their meager possessions. Within an hour, they were on the road. They resurfaced in Indiana a few weeks later. No one from their old town knew where they had gone; they had to find new friends, a new job for his mom, and new living arrangements. This type of uprooting was not uncommon to them. It became a way of life, and what Charlie would come to know as normal.

Charlie's time in Indiana was an introduction to a life of crime, as he moved with the edges of society and was more than willing to assist where he could. His role models and associates were thoroughly steeped in a disregard for the law, ever seeking out new ways to violate community statutes. They involved themselves in any kind of scheme they could find if it made them some money. Charlie learned how to steal cars, pick pockets, burglarize homes and businesses, fence stolen property, and deal drugs.

In one story he told me, Charlie met some underworld figures to whom he intended to sell some guns he had acquired. His collection of pistols was secreted in a potato sack he was clutching. As he and his contacts went out to a houseboat to conduct the transaction, Charlie noticed that there were no firing pins in the guns. He was so afraid that the buyers would not let him escape with his life for deceiving them, even though he never intended to, that he stumbled out a window, fell into the water, and swam for freedom.

He tried his hand at pimping in Indiana, though he was not very successful at it at this point in his life. He also held money and drugs for others. Somewhere along the way, he picked up the guitar and become somewhat proficient at it. I was spellbound as I listened to his many tales of his childhood and his entry into lawlessness.

In time, I let down my guard completely and began to accept everything he said. He had no reason to lie to me or to exaggerate his exploits, I rationalized. I sat on no parole board and was not part of the system. Besides, Charlie trusted me just as I trusted him. The more he shared, the more I felt free to share my own story with him. Soon, I told him all the embarrassing details of my childhood, my disappointments and failures, as well as my dreams and aspirations. We were growing closer and closer by the hour and by the story.

Charlie's life never got any easier, he told me. His mom was arrested for armed robbery and sentenced to prison while he was still young. His life became a succession of institutions, none treating him well. He never seemed to belong anywhere. He longed for the freedom he had experienced with his mother, even though that freedom came part and parcel with frequent abandonment. The group homes, foster homes, and other institutions he was paraded through, each had their own set of dehumanizing rules. He attempted to escape from every place that ever housed him.

Charlie had a great deal of anger built up toward his mother. It was apparent to me that she wasn't a capable parent. She didn't provide for Charlie: not materially and certainly not emotionally. She gave him away or left him with others, again and again. The scars of abandonment were apparent. To be fair, Charlie's mom was only a child herself when she gave birth to him. She had no interest in raising him, and no one gave her much support either.

Despite the resentment, Charlie really loved his mother, I could tell. It was evident in his words and in the expression he put into his words. He wanted more from her. He needed more, but he never got it.

Once out of prison, Charlie's mom reclaimed her son and set about the business of raising him. Shortly thereafter, however, she resumed her pattern of repeatedly dropping him off at relatives or neighbors. She abandoned him to a foster home and later to a group home. Even when he escaped from the foster home, and traveled back to her, she wasn't glad to see him, as he had envisioned. She took him straight back. By the time he achieved adulthood, Charlie's rage was broad and profound. No one should be surprised by his wrath born out of the chaotic childhood he was forced to endure.

While held at a boy's camp in Washington DC, Charlie had his first homosexual encounter, he told me. It happened in a shower. He said that he was quite naïve at the time. This older boy forced himself on young Charlie. He hated the experience. It made him feel dirty and worthless. It was one more instance of another person earning his trust, only to betray him. It was another reminder to him to not let others get close to him emotionally, and to not trust other people. In a few years, Charlie would be the aggressor when he, while incarnated, attacked another inmate, put a knife to his throat, and anally raped him.

At some boy's camp, Charlie got into a fight during a recreation session in the yard. The other boy fell hard on the ground, hit his head, and died. The coroner ruled that they boy had died of a brain aneurism so no charges were filed. Charlie claimed that he fought in self defense, the other boy being larger and tougher. In Charlie's mind, he was the victim; the deceased opponent got what he had coming.

Charlie related to me how he stole a doctor's car to escape this camp. Several miles from the institution, he crashed the vehicle, and fled on foot. He attempted to escape from there many times. Sometimes he would be successful in his escape attempts, eluding authorities for weeks at a time. More often, he admitted, the attempts were useless. Not only did he not escape, he incurred the scorn and retribution of the institution for his behavior.

Charlie became adept at stealing cars before he was 13 years of age.

He learned what models were valuable to his connections and what ones could be quickly fenced through theft rings. Sports cars, while being very expensive, were less popular because they were more difficult to conceal and resell. Mid-sized cars and mid-range priced vehicles were the most lucrative to steal. They could be moved without too many questions, and they brought a return high enough to make the effort profitable.

Charlie learned to move the cars across the state to new towns where the cars wouldn't be recognized. In time, when he became more trusted, Charlie was instructed in the intricacies of moving cars across state lines. He was open to learning anything that would be helpful, and he was a good student of the street. He was a quick study of what he needed to know to protect himself, figuring that the most important information that he could ever learn was anything that would aid him in his survival.

While stealing cars and running them across state lines, someone suggested taking cars down to Mexico where there was great demand and where fewer questions were asked. He tried it and found it extremely profitable. On one occasion, he had a row of hot cars parked on a street in Arizona, near the border to Mexico. He would drive a car across the border, park it and trudge back to pick up the next. On a good day, he could steal and move four automobiles out of the country.

Manson attempted to become a matador, at some point. While in Mexico, he met a man who was born and raised in Spain and who ran a bull-fighter training camp. The fighter saw that Charlie was young and very quick. His slight stature may also have been a plus. In broken English, the fighter invited Charlie to attend the camp and learn how to become a bull fighter. Charlie expressed interest and promised that he would come.

When Charlie showed up at the man's ranch, he saw a group of children lined up outside of the training facility.

"Buenos Dios," the bull fighter called out to the children.

"Buenos Dios," the children replied in unison.

Once inside with the children, Charlie found no bulls, just a few shabbily-clothed Mexicans and a dilapidated sawhorse decorated to look like a bull. Charlie complained. He had no intension of joining a group of neighborhood kids to fight against a pretend bull. The matador explained to him that before someone can be a matador and fight a real bull, he must learn all there is to learn about posture, moves, dress, and performance: it might take a person many years before he was ready for a real bull. This situation displeased Charlie so much that he wandered away from the training camp never to return.

While he sojourned in Mexico, he was warned to not consume any water. He was told stories about Montezuma's revenge, the diarrhea that visitors incurred from microscopic microbes within the country's water. This greatly troubled Manson and was one experience that led him to a deep concern for the environment. How could such a beautiful country have such a polluted water supply? Or, more accurately, how could people so abuse the land as to allow the water to become so filthy? He continued to lose respect for people. Even animals are cleaner than this, Charlie realized.

Charlie also visited Los Angeles around that time. He gathered a few women and sent them out to the streets. He learned the finer points of being a pimp from other, more experienced, criminals, he explained to me. He enjoyed earning money off the labor of someone else. He expressed no remorse or regret to me for taking advantage of the women or of sending them to participate in a vile and repugnant activity. "Usually, they were okay with it," was all Manson could say for the women's experience.

Charlie told me that during a trip to a pawnshop in Los Angeles, he realized a lifelong dream of owning a quality guitar. He had been collecting some good sums of cash from the women he prostituted, and from setting up illegal gambling venues, so money was no longer an issue. He was able to own cars and always had cash with him. On a walk one afternoon, he passed a pawn shop that had a guitar package on display in the window. He entered the store and spoke with an older employee who received him with great skepticism.

"May I help you?" the man queried.

"I'm interested in the guitar in your window. What's it cost?"

"That one is $100 and it includes picks and a case." It was an 8-string Gibson in pristine condition.

Charlie pulled a wad of bills from his pocket. He regularly carried twenties, fifties, and hundreds at this time of his life. His one dollar bills and change were always awarded to street people in need.

He peeled off a one hundred dollar bill and handed it to the employee who, in turn, gathered the guitar and case. After taking the instrument from the man, Charlie peeled off another $100 bill and handed it to him.

"You already paid for the guitar, man," countered the elderly pawnshop employee, who could scarcely believe that this shabbily dressed youngster could afford the first one hundred dollars.

"That is for you." Charlie explained. "Go and buy your wife or girlfriend a fine dinner. I know that things are bad. Everywhere, you hear bad news, wars, and killings. I hope this will give you a good day."

"Well, thank you," the man said in shock. "It's good people like you who give me hope for this world." Charlie found a quiet place on the sidewalk, opened the case, and began to strum the Gibson.

That purchase may have signaled his transition into adulthood. It fed his dream of becoming a popular musician, and gave him the resolve to master his new instrument.

Chapter 6
Charlie Loves Mother Nature

"Look deep into nature, and then you will understand everything better."
Albert Einstein

By inspecting his artwork, you can tell that animals are very important to Charlie. In fact, they are his reason to live. If you heard him speak about wild mammals and bugs, you might conclude that he was crazy. You might think that he has been down too long. But this is merely the way his mind works. He cares about animals, plants and the entire natural realm. He loves nature: anything that is not human is important to him.

He couldn't have cared less for human beings, however. He considered people to be no more than meatballs, or hunks of flesh that often did more harm than good. The human race, to him, was a bother, a nuisance, and a waste of space. He often criticized people for being brain dead or for belonging to a group of mindless followers. He pointed out that people did things that were so horrible that no animal would even consider them. Animals never caused a holocaust, never went to war over an insult, and never killed anything it didn't intend to eat. His distain for people was palpable.

By contrast, his veneration of nature was essentially religious. His philosophy was similar to that of the Native Americans who were reverent of animals and carefully grounded in respect for Mother

Earth. If we all had such concern, it became clear to me, we wouldn't see so much pollution, we wouldn't have to contend with the number of cases of cancer we now see, and the people of the world would be much happier. Just think what our world would be like if it were greener, more oxygenated, and possessed cleaner water!

It is not that we are unaware of what we are doing to the planet. The excuse of ignorance may have been an acceptable defense of our actions 80 or 100 years ago. Today, we know beyond a shadow of a doubt all that we are doing to our streams, lakes and oceans. We are well aware of the impact we are having on our world, yet we continue to pollute and ravage the earth with few restraints.

Charlie taught me this and much more about our natural world. He was vocal about his concerns. "There's only one world, I know," he explained. "If we took the time to look, listen, and learn, we'd find out so much from our mistakes. You don't have to go to college or earn an AA degree to know that what we are doing to Mother Earth is inexcusable. We have the power to make a difference now before it's not too late. The signs are there that Mother Earth is dying.

"Sure, we can pretend we don't see it or know about it," Charlie continued, "but we are only fooling ourselves and lying to each other. If our president has the power to shut down the New York Stock Exchange, and all federal, state, and local offices, then he has the power to make some real changes. If he can order the flag to half staff for the death of a former president or to honor service to the country, there is no reason that he cannot order massive changes to take place universally, changes that will remove the pollution and stop the killing of animals."

He asked me around the same time what I would do if there was no more water to drink. I thought about his question and replied that I would have to rob a convenience store and takes its soda and other drinks. I also suggested digging a well out in the desert, far from others who might try to take the water. I thought that this was what he wanted to hear; I had answered him well, I was certain.

Charlie corrected me, informing me that we should collect wine, since it does not go bad after a short period of time. He was thinking big and said that we should gather barrels and barrels of wine and hide them in a tunnel deep under the mountains. The tunnels could also house tons and tons of food that would not spoil, such as powders and canned goods. He scared me when he said that if someone came around, he would have to kill him to protect the stash. "Either it's him or me," he declared. I asked him about the others and their fate. He replied, "There's no THEM." He wanted me to know what he would do, and also to teach me what to do in that situation. Perhaps, he was training me for future events, an apocalypse that has not yet happened.

Environmentalism was important to Charlie. He regularly spoke of animals and nature, even when sequestered far from any natural setting. Charlie's speech was punctuated with the acronym "ATWA." This encapsulated his philosophy of life, at least on an ecological level. ATWA stands for, "Air, Trees, Water, and Animals." Charlie was a rabid environmentalist years before it was popular to be concerned about the world around us. While some in the hippy movement espoused a concern for the environment, for fighting against pollution, animal cruelty, and the extinction of animals and plants, Charlie made it the centerpiece of his philosophy. Charlie cared more for pristine nature than he did for life itself.

Because Charlie was so often disappointed by people, abused by people, and hated by people, he always felt more comfortable in the presence of animals and plants. His days at the Spahn movie ranch and other remote locations allowed him to retreat from the world of people and find a refuge in the great outdoors. Charlie still longed for a remote, natural place to live and enjoy.

Charlie taught that we will pay for our neglect of the environment. Because people have been abusing the natural elements of our world for so long, we will in time reap the reward of all we have damaged. He foresaw a day when people would muck around in the waste and pollution that they have created. It may not be until our children's children's day, but we will suffer, he believed. He was not inclined to discuss water treatment plants or responsible tree farming. These did not fit into his apocalyptic vision of the future. He spoke to me often of the demise of the human race.

Charlie viewed himself as a savior of plants and animals. Only he, the advocate for an environment that can't verbalize its many ailments, could save nature. He alone cried out on behalf of the natural world, he believed. At times, he was at the edge of despair thinking that it was

66

too late for us to help the world, that too much time had transpired, and too much damage had already been done.

Charlie taught me that air pollution is a terrible plight for our skies. With foreign substances, some unnatural, floating in the atmosphere, we risk lung disease, poisoned lakes, deforestation, and mass extinctions. Because we live in an atmosphere that we can't escape, to pollute the air is to kill ourselves. The first A in ATWA stands for air, the most important element of our world to be at risk from pollution.

Trees (abbreviated by "T") comprise second place in Manson's list of priorities. They enable us to breathe through their vital role in photosynthesis. To cut down a tree is to damage the earth and to send us hurling toward the disastrous end of Easter Island. When it was suggested to him that for every tree that is cut and cultivated for human consumption two be planted, Charlie went ballistic. He was not interested in discussion. Every 400 year old tree supports life that cannot be replaced by two seedlings, he raged. "Trees are our lungs," he proclaimed more than once.

Similarly, water must be protected (The "W" in ATWA), according to Charlie's philosophy. We need water to drink. Animals can't survive without access to clean steams and lakes. If we don't protect our water supplies, animals and people are doomed.

This raised some questions in my mind. If water was so important to him, I wondered, why did he talk so much about deserts? Why did he move to Death Valley, one of the most arid places in the world, immediately before being arrested for his part in murders? I concluded that despite its lack of moisture, deserts held an appeal for Charlie because they are mostly free of human interference. I suspected that he believed that water could be discovered or hidden even in a remote desert.

Animals, to Charlie, the final "A" of his motto, do not include people. That animals must be protected was a profound self-evident tenet in his philosophy of life. He at all times portrayed himself as being one with the environment, not unlike an American Indian. He told me that he had Indian blood in him. He also told me about the time he spent with Native Americans, and how he had been profoundly shaped by them, even if he was not a full native himself.

To Charlie, humans are less important than animals. They are superfluous actually, even detrimental to life on the planet. They wreak havoc with the world. Animals and plants seem to be able to co-exist. By contrast, humans work hard to destroy the environment and its ecological balances, take what they do not need, and leave garbage and chemical pollution behind. Many groups of people cannot even coexist with other similar groups. The world would be better if humans did not exist, never had existed. I wondered sometimes whether Charlie had really studied the situation, and knew and understood the positive and negative effects of humans in the world. I am much more positive in my outlook than my friend. Nevertheless, I saw the importance of what he said.

I have heard the arguments against Charlie: that his philosophy is a convenient way to induce guilt and fear in others, that it is a way to excuse his own actions, and that it is a means to give him something to hold sacred in light of his loathing of all humans including himself. I don't buy it, though. Despite his pessimism, Charlie has much to teach the world about the importance of nature, and the natural processes of our world.

More than once, Charlie commented on the profound difference between the two of us, my optimistic look at the world and at people, contrasting significantly with his hopeless outlook and despair of humankind. I think I'm not all that different from Charlie, however. Like him, I think we need to protect our world from harm and disaster.

I listened to Charlie for hours as he espoused his care and concern for the world and all that is in it. I engaged him in discussions about the air, trees, water, and animals. I couldn't find fault in what he said. It fit into my own understanding of the environment. Who can argue with the threats of pollution?

Always, I was mesmerized by his speech. I could easily understand a group of wayward teens falling in love with, and following, this man. I have to admit that in some strange way I became very attracted to him. I could understand the power he had over others for he had that power over me. It now made sense to me that the mere mention of his name could invoke feelings of awe and wonder. More than a few times, I had dropped his name to increase my own status with others. Inmates and guards would all stop and give me their undivided attention when I shared with them something Charlie had told me, or when I showed them something that he had given me. I began to see the beauty of Charles Manson as a human being. The old man can help people use their brain and see things the way they are, I marveled. Is he the smartest person I had ever met? Maybe, he was the smartest person in the whole world. I began to follow him in my own way.

Later, even in the quietness of my own mind, when I reviewed the things he shared with me, I came to the conclusion that he was a great man. Was he egotistical? Yeah. At times he could be, but who isn't? In general, Charlie was a down to earth man, a beautiful person that every man, woman, and child could learn something from to make this a better world. The most profound thing he ever said to me, something that for me crystallized his importance was this: "We are one. There is no you, me, him, they, them. There is only one!" I did not know the full implication of this wisdom, but I knew it was deep. I trusted him that in the depth of his profundity, he was really, really smart.

One of the most troubling events in all of his life, Charlie explained to me, was a time when he was forced to kill a rabbit. Tears welled up in his eyes as he recounted to me the tale of horror that no child should have to experience.

When Charlie was still a child of eight, his mother was arrested and convicted for an armed robbery she had committed with her brother. While the two were in prison, there was nowhere for Charlie to go. His mother decided to put him in a foster home when no friend or family member agreed to take him.

The foster home was a large one, housing ten abandoned children in addition to Charlie and the elderly couple who hosted them all. It was evident to Charlie that the foster parents knew how to make good use of the children's abilities. The foster mother ruled the home like a dictator. She expected everyone to get up at five o'clock in the morning to participate in the chores, which included milking cows, collecting eggs, picking vegetables, and cleaning animal pens. The woman meantime churned her own butter, cooked all the meals, cleaned the house, and mended all the clothing.

Her industriousness was matched only by her cruelty, however. One morning, the woman told young Charles to go down to the basement to kill a rabbit. He was ordered to slit the animal's throat, skin its hide, and wash the pelt in warm water. Charlie resisted and resisted, trying to find a way out of harming this poor, innocent creature. He felt bad for it. When he could find no more excuses and had come to the end of his pleading, the woman's command ruled the day. Charlie placed the knife against the bunny's throat and ended its life.

"The rabbit shrieked and shrieked," Charlie told me, choking back the tears. "There was blood everywhere and it kept crying out." I noted that this was something like a scene out of the movie, "Silence of the Lambs," where Jodie Foster's character, Clarice Starling, had to endure the screams of slaughtered lambs. It appeared to be similar, except, unlike Clarice, Charlie had to actually deliver the violence and not just witness it. It was evident to me that this event tormented Charlie. He was still troubled by it all these years later.

"Why did she make me do that?" Manson wanted to know. "How could she be so cruel?" At the tender age of eight, he was too sensitive and caring to engage in such a violent act. It was yet another episode that soured his view of human nature. Over time, experiences like this caused him to become deeply concerned about animals and bitter toward the human race.

"I don't like humans much because they're brain dead," he once told me. "Just look at all the filth in this world, smog, polluted waters, deforestation all over the world." Charlie held back none of his hatred of people. "We're all meatballs, hamburgers, milkshakes, and French fries. It's as easy to be eaten as it is to go into McDonalds and order a meal and devour it!"

To deal with the damage that people inflict on the natural world, Charlie created what he called, "The People's International Court of Retribution." It consisted of a judge (Charlie), jury (Charlie), and executioner (Charlie). Sessions were held without warning whenever Charlie felt so inclined. We, the general public, are the spectators to the Charles Manson brand of justice, but only if we have upheld his high standards in protecting the animals and environment.

With great flourish and passion, Charlie would present evidence, declare his rulings and pass sentence. Others might have considered him crazy for what he said. It didn't matter to him. His only concern was for ATWA, air, trees, water and animals. His distain for those who harmed the world was evident in the threats he breathed. He promised a fate worse than his own upbringing, worse than the way the defendant had treated the animal or the air, worse than the greatest punishment ever meted out against him. I enjoyed listening to him as he held court against some new infraction or against some group within society that disappointed him. He could get so enraged and animated. One day it would be the state of California on mock trial; the next it would be some inmate who made a derogatory comment about an animal; another day it was society in general for its neglect of conservation. He could never execute the harsh sentence that would inevitably be the outcome of the trial, of course. Still, it was fun to watch--and highly entertaining.

When he was not holding court, he was talking about animals. Even the wellbeing of a spider or moth garnered Charlie's attention, as became evident during our discussions or visits to the yard. It was a rare occasion that Charlie took the opportunity to go to the yard, but when he did, it was all about the animals he saw, even the smallest of creatures.

When he was not holding court, he was talking about animals. Even the wellbeing of a spider or moth garnered Charlie's attention, as became evident during our discussions or visits to the yard. It was a rare occasion that Charlie took the opportunity to go to the yard, but when he did, it was all about the animals he saw, even the smallest of creatures.

It was still dark outside when a beefy guard with an oversized uniform tapped on my door with his baton. "Mendez, are you going out to morning yard?" He enquired.

"No," I refused without looking up from my bed. I was too tired to get up.

As I lowered my head back down to the make-shift pillow I had created out of the state-issued blanket, I heard the same tapping at the next cell. "Charlie, are you going out to morning yard?" The guard had been around long enough to know what everyone in the cell house knew: Charlie did not like to go out of his cell for anything, not the shower, not the yard, and not just to stretch his legs. In fact, if there were a fire on the cell block, and the inmates were to be evacuated one cell at a time, there is a good chance that Charlie would remain in his cell and refuse an offer to leave.

Sometimes, guards have to take extraordinary measures to remove

71

an uncooperative inmate from a cell. When a prisoner refuses an order to leave his cell, the guards take immediate action. First, they will tell the inmate that he can either cooperate and do it the easy way, or they will be forced to do it the hard way. Upon a second refusal, the guards will gather in number, enough to overwhelm the prisoner, and then spray him with mace. If there is still no cooperative response, they will open his cell door and rush him. Wearing hockey helmets, plastic face guards over gas masks, heavy chest protectors, elbow pads, knee pads, and shin pads, they will cower behind a Plexiglas shield. They want to protect themselves in the event that the hostile inmate has a spear or knife secreted in his cell, or can assault them with a gaseous or liquid weapon. One way or another, the prison ensures that its orders are carried out. Unless an inmate is mentally ill, or desirous of a fight, he will eventually comply to avoid the physical confrontation.

On this particular morning, Charlie was not required to come out of his cell. He had been invited. "I don't know," was his reply to the invitation. "I don't like people coming in my cell and stealing from me." What he was talking about was a mystery to me. He had not left his cell in weeks. No one could possibly have taken anything from him. Perhaps he was referring to an event a long time ago. Maybe he was imagining the thefts.

After a few moments of deliberation, Charlie gave the rare reply to the guard, "Yeah, I'll go out." He added a condition. "I'll go out if you make sure that no one goes in my cell while I'm in the yard."

"Sure, Charlie," the guard replied. "I promise you I won't let no one go inside your cell. That's my word and my word is my bond and my bond is my life." These words of promise are exactly what Charlie would frequently say to others. By using them, the guard revealed that he was hip, and that he would protect the old man. He showed that he was a person who listened and who respected Charlie. This seemed to put the old man at ease.

I had emerged from my bed by this time. As cold as it was on the floor, I wanted to witness this spectacle. Charlie had not been out of his cell in over three months. He had once told me, "Willie, I can stay in my cell for a year straight and never leave. Other people start to lose their minds because they are weak minded, but not me!" Finally, I would witness him leaving his cell after more than three months.

The guard moved to the top of his door to unlock a special red padlock, secured in place in the unlikely event that all the cell doors opened up accidentally. Because he is a high risk inmate, Charlie is not allowed even the remotest chance of leaving his cell by accident. No one wanted Charlie wandering around the prison. The security lock also protected him from any attack by another inmate. The beefy guard unlocked the tray slot of Charlie's cell, allowing the steel plate that covered the opening to fall with a clank.

From my window, I could see two hands emerge from the cell. They were white and bony, engulfing nails that were long and unkempt. He resembled what I would expect in a wild man who had been abandoned in the jungle, or a psychiatric patient locked up to protect himself and society. Cuffs were secured around his wrists before the guard called for the opening of his cell: "Twenty-seven! Two! Seven!" The tower guard who was at the control board opened Charlie's cell so that the old man could step out of the only room he had known in weeks. I noticed his long, shaggy hair and his beard that flopped down over his chest. A wrinkled yellow jump suit hung from his small frame. He made no effort to adjust his clothing or smooth out its wrinkled surface. On his feet, I observed well-worn black tennis shoes.

"Have a good yard, Charlie," I yelled as I banged on my window. As he turned, I saw him smile at me. He appeared to be free of any worry about an invasion of his cell while he was away. As he shuffled toward the tier door, I concluded that he was not going out to the yard in weakness. After thirty-five years of incarceration, he had the right to do whatever he wanted, whenever he wanted. Too, no one better criticize him or speak ill of him while he was gone. I determined that I would monitor the conversations that took place in his absence. I was happy to note that no one said anything disrespectful to him as he left the unit. It was still really early in the morning: breakfast would not be served for another half hour. Charlie could be gone for as long as three hours, I knew.

I turned my attention to cleaning myself up for the day. At my stainless steel sink, I grabbed a bar of soap and starting washing up in a rush of hot water. I brushed my teeth and began to fold my blankets when I heard the breakfast guard approach from the door that led to two sections called lower A and lower B.

"Chow time," the breakfast guard announced. "Uncover your lights and stand at your door, or I'll pass you by." I knew that if I didn't obey, I would miss breakfast and would not receive a bag lunch. I could not wait until dinner that was not due to be served for another ten hours!

I recognized the guard. He was an ex-marine drill sergeant who had seen action in Vietnam. He was what you would call, "a true Marine Devil Dog." He was firm in the orders that he gave to everyone. He always kept his boots clean and shiny, as nicely polished as his gear; his uniform was always immaculate.

He yelled to the tower guard his staccato order, "Open twenty six! Two! Six!" He jammed my breakfast tray through the meal slot. As I received it, I surveyed its contents: scrambled eggs, beans, two tortillas, two hot sauce packets, grits, two packets of imitation sugar, a packet of state coffee, and one half pint of milk. The eggs were still steaming. Because it was Tuesday, I also received some fresh fruit juice. Sometimes, the juice would be substituted with stewed prunes or stewed apples. On rare occasions, we would find stewed apricots. But not today.

I received my sack lunch at the same time. I opened it to inspect the contents, not really anticipating anything out of routine. I found what I had come to expect: a bologna sandwich, an apple, chips, and some graham crackers. Lunch never changed. Never.

The guard went to Charlie's cell. After carefully setting a meal in the cell, he placed a second tray over top of it, upside down, to keep Charlie's food as warm as possible in his absence.

It was going to be a good day, I reasoned. Charlie had gone outside to see some birds, bugs, and plants. He would shower if he dared to do that in the 50 degree weather outside. That would wake him up and refresh him, I thought.

At three hours exactly, the Devil Dog returned with Charlie. For me, it was a joy. It was like seeing a long lost friend again, even though it had been only a few hours since he left. I was happy for him, certain that the trip to the yard was soothing and refreshing. I was feeling happy for myself, too. Here was the most notorious killer in American history, swastika on his forehead, the most dangerous person in our prison—and he was my friend. In his absence, I began to realize how much this man meant to me. His history did not matter to me. Where he had been and what he had been involved with prior to our friendship did not affect me and our relationship. I was ecstatic to see him return to me.

I had half expected him to behave like a raving lunatic outside of his cell. It had been so long since he had left it that I didn't know how he might act. He was not affected by his long stay in his cell, it appeared to me: he was calm, walking with a flat-footed shuffle. He had told me he practiced his ability to always be alert and always be nimble on his feet. He knew after so many attempts on his life that he could be attacked at any time. He had also told me about how he practiced every movement. "In prison, you can't take anything for granted," he had warned me. "The only certainty for an inmate is death." Charlie worked hard each day to postpone that inevitability.

It was common knowledge that whoever killed Charles Manson, if someone were able to reach him and carry out that act, would be recorded in history. The murderer's name would be entwined with Charlie's forever and ever. Some no-named lifer who has nothing to look forward to could instantly make a name for himself by bringing about the death of Charles Manson. Because the prison system knew this about Charlie, guards took extra precautions to keep him alive. Yet, they provide no bodyguard service. They have a prison to run and costs to contain. They do what they can to keep each prisoner safe without any guarantees. Sometimes, what they do proves insufficient.

With Charlie, there is more incentive to keep him alive than with other, typical inmates. No prison official, guard or administrator, wants to be responsible for the death of such a high profile inmate. Not on their watch! The staff also does not want their prison to be the location of his murder. That would not bode well for the politics of prison funding or the institution's reputation. Daily, the conflict played out between the no-name inmates desiring to gain historical significance and vigilant guards attempting to uphold the prison's safety record. In the center of this storm of conflict, Charlie's life hung in the balance.

When Charlie was back in his cell, he asked me, out of the guard's earshot, "Did anyone come in my cell while I was gone?"

"No, Charlie." I responded. "It's all good. They know better than to lie to you like that!" I wasn't sure if he asked out of paranoia or out of a sense of protection of his turf. Probably both.

"Did you see any birds out there?" I changed the subject.

CHAPTER 6

"Yes, I seen some birds flying around, some ants walking around, and I seen a black widow, too!" He was referring to a black widow spider that had been spotted in the Section-A Yard, or Yard One as it is frequently called. It lived in a crack in the cement at the far end of the lot. In the shelter provided by the crack, in a pile of leaves above a dirt floor, it had built a three-foot web. It would gracefully emerge from its hole to capture and eat any unfortunate insects that got entangled in the web. It could manage a grasshopper if it had to, even one that was ten times its weight. Charlie was particularly eager to talk that day and filled me in on all the events of his trip outside.

Two days later, it was my turn to go out. "Mendez, you want to go out to the yard, today?" A young guard queried me.

"Yeah," I replied. I was in need of some fresh air and different scenery.

"OK, be ready in five minutes." He commanded as he left the section. He appeared less sure of himself than the veteran guards.

Five minutes later, he returned and unlocked my tray slot. I slid my hands through the opening and waited as I was cuffed. The door opened as the guard yelled, "B-Section, twenty eight! Two! Eight! " I turned around and walked toward the yard. Because it was still a little chilly, I requested and received a jean jacket to be used only in the yard. I glanced toward Charlie's cell as I walked passed it, and noticed him wearing his state-issued, black reading glasses. I tipped my head back in greeting. He returned the gesture.

Once outside, I drew in the cool fresh air. The sky was clear. The birds had apparently fled for shelter from the strong breeze. You cannot prepare for this cold when you are confined to a cell all day, every day. You can think about it and attempt to prepare your mind for the experience, but the reality is too palpable for the imagination. I shuddered against the stiff wind, quickening my pace to provide some warmth.

When my allotted three hours had elapsed, I stood waiting for my escorting officer. Another guard noticed me and asked whether I would like some books. I asked him what he had. He listed a few different titles, including a murder mystery and a military book. I said, "I will take those two," indicating two books to his left.

He handed them to me and added, "Charlie really likes you. He don't like most people." I agreed, pointing out that most people judge

76

him by what they hear in the news.

"I accept him for who he is," I boasted.

"Yeah, well, I like the old man, too," the guard assured me. He smiled. "He can sure tell stories, can't he?"

"Yes, he's been around a while." I turned to walk away. When I got to my section block, I noticed that Charlie was at his window. He smiled at me while he did something with his hands. It occurred to me that he was weaving something, not unlike the spider in the yard. That was an interesting metaphor, I thought: Charlie was just like the spider, weaving a web and attempting to catch something. I wondered what he was creating and what he meant to catch.

I had to drop the books on the floor once I arrived at my cell. The tray slot was only six inches by eighteen inches. I always had to carefully maneuver my six-foot, 230-pound frame so I could slide my hands through. After I was uncuffed, I washed my hands and wiped down the books. The cuffs were always dirty and God only knew where the books had been. I like to keep myself clean and a prison cell offers no protection from germs.

Soon Charlie was banging on the wall. "Boxcar!"

"Yeah, Charlie. What's up?" I replied.

"How was your yard?" He was as interested in my time outside as I was in his.

"Oh, it was really nice, Charlie. It was a little too cold, but it was okay." I elaborated. "I saw some bugs and a moth. The birds weren't out. The moth was the biggest one I'd ever seen."

"What did you do with it?" He wanted to know. His tone of voice was firmer and more serious than I had heard from him before.

"I watched it fly over the wall," I lied. I had no interest in arousing his anger.

"Oh, that's good. That's good." The old man said in a tone that resonated of a child's fascination mixed with that of an approving parent.

I knew that he considered all animals, even moths, sacred. I didn't have the heart to tell him that the moth was dying and I fed it to some ants. I figured it made no difference to the moth. The ants would have found it eventually. I felt bad for lying to my friend, but not bad enough to incur his wrath. I didn't want to have to sit and explain it to him either. I rationalized that I had helped the ants, not killed the moth. I'm not sure that Charlie would interpret events that way, and I didn't mean to find out.

Later in the day, I came to see how profound Charlie's concern was for the natural world. He asked me about the moth again: "It went over the wall?"

"Yes, Charlie. It did go over the wall." I said, repeating my lie.

Perhaps picking up on my falsehood, he growled, "Because anyone who messes with the bugs will be cursed and what they do to the bugs will be done to them!"

For a long time afterwards, I stopped killing bugs. Not so much out of fear, but out of the love and respect that I had toward Charlie. I cared about nature, but no one could care as deeply as Charlie.

Chapter 7
Keep it Real

"In poverty and other misfortunes of life, true friends are a sure refuge."
Aristotle

Charlie often talked to me about friendship, not just our relationship but the concept in general. He insisted that I understand what it was, what it looked like, and what it took to be a true friend. It seemed like such a simple topic, since everyone learns about friendship about the same time he or she learns to walk, but to Charlie it was much more complex than I thought—and very personal. He spoke of our friendship in the most intimate terms.

"People will hate you as they've hated me all of these years," he said. He seemed to be quoting Jesus. "You are famous just by being around me because I have spoken things to you that I never have to any one else.

"Boxcar," he continued. "You are famous now. You're in history." Since I was locked up next to him, since I had furthered a relationship with such a celebrated and feared icon, I guessed he was right. I was not sure what it meant for me, though.

"I don't like people," he went on, "because they are a lot of problems, and they've brought me a lot of problems. I don't need any friends because friends are a responsibility.

"There was this Hawaiian guy." Charlie's tone changed as he began to recount a story he had heard. "He wanted to take his friends with him when he died. He dug a big hole and put a long pole inside of it. He called his friends over and asked them to climb down in the hole and hold up the pole for him. They did what he requested because they were his friends. He pulled out a gun and killed all of them before taking his own life."

"That's what a real friend is about." I said to show Charlie that I had understood his message. "He will lay down his life for his friend. He will do whatever it takes to serve him without thinking twice about whether he'll live or die. A true friend gives to protect those he cares about most: his friends and family members.

"There's no honorable way to die in this fucked up world, Charlie." I added.

"You got that right, Boxcar," Charlie agreed. "I knew there was some reason why I liked you. You're very smart!"

"Thanks, Charlie. You're very smart too, you old man." I laughed at my joke, "ha ha ha." Charlie joined my laughter.

When I had been living next to Charlie for about ten months, I decided that I would show him the depth of my devotion to him and to our friendship. We had been through much together, most of it positive, some of it trying. Despite the tough times, and maybe even because of them, we really did care for one another.

One day, when a guard passed my cell, one with whom I got along reasonably well, I asked him if I could come out of my cell to sweep and mop the tier. He gave me a suspicious look. I could see that he was reviewing in his mind my previous violent acts. He was weighing a decision, while considering whether I was trying to pull something over on him or not. I explained that I wanted to sweep and mop the floor correctly, to make the area a better place in which to live. He acquiesced with a shout to the tower guard. "Close B-section. Then open cell door twenty-six." He must have reasoned that a better living area for me would mean a better work environment for him. I am sure he concluded that if we were happier, his life would be, too.

As I stepped out of my cell, I determined that this was my time to shine. I felt an emotion like no other I had ever experienced. By this time, I cherished Charlie as a father figure and a brother, and I knew the project I was carrying out would make him as proud of me as any father is of his son. I wanted to be successful and have him admire and enjoy my success. The guard who had momentarily left me alone returned with a broom, mop, and pail of hot water. I took the broom from his outstretched hands and began to sweep.

Once I had completed the first tier, I surveyed the pile of dust, dead bugs, tiny rocks, and old food items that I had collected. I knew that there had to be billions of dust mites and germs in my pile. I cringed as I thought about it. The second tier was not as dirty, but I was able to gather another similar pile that nearly turned my stomach.

I lifted the mop the guard had brought out for me. Dipping it in the still scalding water, the first place I set to work was the area of dried soap right in front of Charlie's cell. I looked across at Charlie as I labored over the floor. He smiled a broad, toothless smile which I quickly returned. With each thrust of the mop, I could feel my relationship with Charlie growing. We were getting closer and closer. We knew we had done it: we had stolen the floor. This was our tier. We alone had bragging rights to the entire area, the only piece of the planet over which we had any claim. And we staked our claim.

My job of cleaning the floors only took me about forty-five minutes. The guards were so appreciative of my efforts that they offered me seven lunches that were left over from earlier in the day. They also provided me with extra items from breakfast and dinner. The guards regularly collected these items and used them to reward positive behavior. It was an inexpensive way for them to manage our actions. Their eagerness in providing for me showed me how thankful they were, but I was more interested in pleasing Charlie than in collecting more food.

I had done this for Charlie. I cared about the other guys on the tier and wanted them to have a better living space, but mostly I cared about how it would affect Charlie. The soap was gone; the dust was gone. I knew he could breathe easier now that our floor was immaculate. The bare tier lights reflected off the shiny gray paint of the floor. Gone were the scraps of paper that had once clogged up the drains. Gone also were any last traces of Strawberry from our lives.

I sensed how appreciative Charlie was, even if he didn't put his feelings into words. He showed me a lot of love over the next weeks. Our arguments of the past were no more than distant history. He now knew how deeply I cared about him--and appeared to reciprocate my emotions.

In our friendship, Charlie could be very blunt. He taught me many things, but I didn't always like how he talked to me—not at first. His tone seemed to suggest that he didn't respect me. Over time, I came to see how he really did have my best interests in mind. He was blunt and forthright in order to teach me things I needed to learn. At times, I must admit, I require direct confrontation to accept something I have previously rejected or to learn something new. When I explained to Charlie how I arrived at Corcoran in the SHU, for instance, and detailed how I stabbed my child-molesting cellie, I expected to be praised. I was mistaken.

"You stabbed yourself," Charlie blurted out.

Thinking that he may not have heard me or understood me, I repeated that I stabbed my cell-mate because of what he had done and because of his disrespect for me.

"You stabbed yourself," he said again. He explained that whenever we do acts of violence toward others, we are doing more damage to ourselves. "We might as well stab ourselves as stab someone else," he told me. The results for us are the same.

He had a point, I had to admit. It made me consider my actions and the effect that they were having upon me. I had never stopped to think about my behavior in that way before. Charlie may have saved me from many future violent acts, may have saved me from further episodes of stabbing "myself." I came to appreciate his boldness with me.

Charlie would often say to me, "We are one. There is no you, me, him, they, or them. There is only one!" I heard it over and over until I was sick of hearing it. It became a kind of mantra for him. Whenever I would get angry at someone and vow revenge, whenever someone else's actions irked me, whenever I spoke of an enemy, Charlie tried to get me to see things a different way, "We are one. There is no you, me, him, they, or them. There is only one!" Hearing that phrase impressed upon me the foolishness of all anger I harbored toward others. Over time, Charlie helped soften my rage. As the months went by, whether due to my maturing or the instruction I was receiving from my friend, I felt the urge to strike back and hurt others less and less.

I expressed my love for Charlie in many pranks, often doing things to him just to see what made him tick. He knew I was testing him. I wanted to know the real Charlie. I knew he could talk a good game, but I didn't know whether he backed up his talk in his actions and in his heart of hearts. I wanted to know whether he was as tough as he portrayed himself to be. Before I was incarcerated, I often put others to the test. I especially enjoyed it if some little guy was pretended to be tough. Since I am bulked up to 230 pounds in my 6-foot frame, it is easy for me to stand up to a smaller person. Only those who truly carry street smarts and a mental toughness can impress me.

I liked to fiddle with the lock on Charlie's tray slot as I walked past his cell. I would never do this if he was sleeping. That would violate a cardinal rule in prisons. To wake a sleeping inmate is to disrespect him. Only a truly angry, vengeful inmate will wake another inmate—and he had better be prepared for the consequences. I never wanted to show even the least amount of disrespect to Charlie.

If he was awake, however, and I was feeling mischievous, I would jiggle his lock on the way to my shower. When he would hear it, he would show an immediate and profound fear. He had the look of an animal trapped in a corner. I felt bad for giving him such a fright, especially knowing that his hold on life was so fragile. He had already been the brunt of many attacks, and never knew who wanted to do him harm. Still, by teasing him this way, I had a front row seat to the show of his reaction. He demonstrated fear, but he still was one of the boldest, toughest, and mentally strongest people I have ever met. I could tell that Charlie was never unraveled by fear.

He spoke to me often about fear, not about what made him afraid, but about the need to overcome the fears in our lives. He claimed to fear nothing. "Boxcar," he once said. "I'm the man who will go and face the fear I have. I'd do that instead of running from it. To overcome my fear is to challenge my fear, whatever fear is, or whatever it means. I'll eat fear for breakfast, lunch and dinner. I'll make fear my friend instead of my enemy. I digest it and conquer it." He spoke in the soft and philosophical tone of John Lennon.

Once, he told me that you have to keep the fear level up. "Fear is life." He said. "If others don't fear you, they won't respect you. But if they fear you and are afraid of what you might do to them, they will give you all the respect in the world!"

These were no mere words to Charlie. I saw firsthand how that played out around the prison. I saw so many inmates or guards with fear in their eyes, or fear in their body language, as they spoke to, or about, Charles Manson. If they had the chance to talk with him and get to know him, I have no doubt that they would mellow out. They acted on edge, as if something could happen at any moment, simply by hearing the name Charles Manson or seeing him pass by.

I saw Charlie build up that fear level in others in some pretty crazy ways, too. He could stare down an inmate or guard, put on a silly smile, or if he was overly tired, he could growl like a hungry junkyard dog. I saw guards leave the building after hearing one of Charlie's growls. Others have quickly offered Charlie something or asked him to show them his artwork in an effort to diffuse the situation. It seems that everyone walked on egg shells around Charlie. "Keep the fear level up," Charlie would tell me. It was a game to him.

Once, he made a voodoo doll that resembled a guard that he despised. He said some evil words, played on his bongos, and pricked it with some pins. As far as I know, the guard never knew about it—fortunately for the both of them.

"I want to teach you things, too, Charlie," I confided one day, "but how can I teach something to someone who knows everything already?"

"We are all babies," Charlie opined, "and we learn when we are willing to learn, or we don't learn. Whether we have learned something already or not, we will pick up something out of whatever lesson comes our way."

When he spoke this, it became clear to me that Charlie was a born leader. He had confidence and charisma. He was always talking about something new and interesting. He knew what made people tick. Even here, he would not put me down, even though I claimed to know nothing that he didn't already comprehend. He was a brilliant leader who protected those he led.

Occasionally, I would nitpick at Charlie to gauge his reaction and better understand him. He did not get mad at me very often. It would take a lot of abuse before he would yell at me. Usually, he would just laugh at me or mock me for trying to get his goad.

I learned to never underestimate him, however. He always had some game going. Either he was trying to get the guards to do something or convince one of the other inmates to carry out a project for him.

It was funny to see him dance the dance of manipulating others. I began to see him as a "con-troller." He was a convict, or "con," and he was always trying to control others, so I coined the term "con-troller." Being around him was like watching a wrestling match. I never knew what the next moves would be, but I knew it would be fun to watch. It was always entertaining to be housed right next to Charlie.

I got to see a lot of the different faces of Charles Manson, too. He seemed to have different personalities that he was able to call upon at will. Depending on who he was speaking with, he could be coy, aggressive, witty, dangerous, insane, and even demure. I began to see how he often role-played simply to get someone to do something for him.

Charlie and I didn't always get along. We had our share of disagreements, often annoying each other in one way or another. If anyone tells you that they always get along very well with their cell-mate or friend in neighboring cell, call him or her a liar. No one can live in such confined quarters and not erupt from time to time. All inmates, whether they are male, female, adult, juvenile, or whatever, no matter where they are held, at a federal institution, local holding cell, or state prison, are treated like cages animals. Even zoos provide more living space for their residents.

Inmates come in all shapes and sizes, backgrounds, religious beliefs, and bad habits. Putting them in close proximity doesn't remove these differences; indeed, it magnifies them. Generally, the toughest part of prison time is handling the diversity of humanity that is found behind bars. It would be hard enough to cope with so many "normal" people confined to tiny rooms. An average population would probably be easier to survive. Behind bars, you do not find typical people or a cross section of society. You encounter men who through circumstances or bad choices find themselves on the wrong side of the law. Not only are there a variety of personalities, nationalities, and religious persuasion, in prison there are multiple personalities, dominators, manipulators, and those who prey on others. As it is, it's amazing that there aren't more fights and greater animosities.

When Charlie and I got into it, when we would really have a row, he would go to the guards and ask them to do things to bother me. It really got under my skin when he would talk to a guard to whom he was close and have that guard dog me. Some guards would deny me yard privileges, serve me a small tray at breakfast or dinner, cut my shower short, or lose my canteen slip. I always knew that it was Charlie behind it; it had his name written all over it. I can handle some harassment from guards. That is to be expected behind bars. Convicts learn pretty quickly to swing with the punches. What annoyed me most was the fact that Charlie went to the guards in the first place. How cowardly is that? He is supposed to be so strong, so fearless, and instead of dealing with me directly, he goes to the authorities to exact revenge. I can only wonder about the cost to Charlie. What did he have to do to repay the guards for my harassment? Did he promise to comply with that guard at a later date? Charlie must have been making deals with the devil. He was playing off both sides of the law.

I saw Charlie cozy up to guards more than once. During the first weeks next to me, he got so obnoxious that I began to suspect that he had put LSD in my food. I didn't know how he could have done that, but the visions that ran through my mind left me no other conclusion. Later, when we weren't talking to each other, I saw him get revenge on me through the guards. He was able to convince them to shortchange me out of food items and throw my mail around the cell (rather than handing it to me). It angered me that he had such power over the guards and the ability to disturb me; it hurt me that he would do those things to me. Fortunately, our disagreements never lasted longer than a day or two. I was glad to work things out with him after each argument. As we discussed our grievances with one another, I reminded myself that in such an unnatural situation as prison, friends are critical for survival.

There are some inmates who will do the laundry for another in exchange for some kind of payment such as coffee, food, or whatever. I could never do that. I was raised to be self-sufficient and to encourage others to be that way too. I wouldn't allow someone else to clean my clothes, nor would I want to clean another's. However, I would have cleaned Charlie's clothes, even his cell, if I had the chance. That is how much I cared for the man. I didn't view him as just another inmate. To me, he was my father, my brother, my guide and guru, a person more important to me than my own family.

There were times I felt obliged to protect Charlie due to his advancing years. It was apparent to me that senility was setting in. The predators behind bars will prey on the weak, all of the weak, including the aged and infirmed. Like many elderly people, Charlie had been abandoned by family, and denied care that he dearly needed.

He was still very alert and very cautious, often overly suspicious and paranoid. I couldn't blame him because of all that he has had to endure. I observed that almost every day someone was talking "shit" about him. If it wasn't an inmate on the tier, or someone from another building passing a note, it was a person from the media communicating through the radio or newspaper. The worst were the comedians who often invoked his name as a synonym for pure evil before hitting a punch line that was never respectful of him. I learned to keep any negative information away from him.

At first, when I told him that I had heard or seen something about him, he would always say, "Yeah? What did they say?" I could tell that it hurt him and infuriated him when I recounted the slight. Over time, I stopped passing on information that I knew would upset him. He didn't need to hear the latest joke or the false bravado of some rookie inmate who had never even met Charlie. On anniversaries of the Tate and La Bianca killings, the number of references to Charlie would always peak. It was especially important at these times for me to remain silent.

I felt very close to Charlie because of the depth of his sharing with me. He had a way of opening himself that at one and the same time revealed him to be vulnerable, yet very, very strong. He could be open, extremely open, sharing some of the disappointments of his life: how others had let him down, how he was abused as a child, and how he never had the support, supervision, and direction he needed as a young boy. Yet, I found out quickly that this sharing couldn't be equated with weakness. Charlie refused to show any form of weakness. "Kindness is not weakness," he often told me. And, to me, he was very, very kind—and generous.

Charlie made it clear to me that if I ever double-crossed him or brought harm to any of his friends, he would be sure to exact his revenge. He never detailed what he would do to me, the same way he seldom fleshed out his threats to others. However, it was impressed upon me that I didn't want to even know what his revenge would look like. He never threatened me directly; he was able to couch his words in hypothetical instances where other people would be the ones who stepped out of line and others would be the recipients of revenge. He seldom took responsibility for violence or threats, but no thinking person could come away from his warnings without the clear message that to bring harm to Charlie was a punishable offense.

Even with the threats looming over me, our friendship could proceed. He had three rules for close friendship that he regularly shared. Friends of Charlie had to:

1) Keep it real
2) Never tell lies, and
3) Be a friend to his friends.

It was almost a gang code, the way he explained it.

By keeping it real, I was never to act phony around him. He wanted to know what was going on, exactly. He forbad me from playing games with him, falsely flattering him, or deceiving him. I'm not sure that he obeyed his own rule. In retrospect, it is possible that this code was part of the grooming to which he subjected others. He had no qualms about playing mind games with me. He had no problems with deceiving others, although not usually directly. By insisting that I keep it real, more than likely he was setting me up to be manipulated by him. At the very least, he was informing me that he was in control of the relationship.

He also never wanted me to lie to him directly. He told me that to lie was to disrespect. He noted that when you lie, you damage your own reputation. "Lies always get revealed sooner or later," he explained.

Charlie's third requirement ensured that his friends were friends with each other. Not that he had all that many close contacts in jail: he didn't. Nevertheless, he insisted that those who were in his inner circle commanded the same respect and deference that he did. I never had any difficulty abiding by this demand. Generally, I don't cross anyone's path unless I must. I'm not well connected enough to afford to be on the wrong side of anyone, especially a powerful icon such as Charlie. If Charlie wanted me to befriend his friends, I was happy to oblige.

Charlie's friends consisted mostly of those celled around him. He spent almost his entire week in his cell. He could if he wanted to, and sometimes did, send messages to other parts of the tier by means of a fish line or relayed message. Most of his communication was to the neighboring cells where he could converse quickly and in some privacy, however. His mail contacts were much more spread out, obviously. He corresponded for months or years with people on the outside. I had no doubt, ever, that he was strongly protected by his friends, whoever they were or wherever they happened to be; therefore, I never sought to harm him or allow any harm to be done to him. I knew my safety depended upon it. With his worldwide contacts, and his media presence, I could not risk being out of his favor. I learned that I would have to be loyal to him until death, even when we were in the throes of disagreement and not talking to one another. Because I cared for him so much, it was not hard labor for me to be committed.

I was educated about political movements through my relationship with Charlie, even though it was not a formal education. Through our friendship, he taught me how the world works. He impressed upon me the need for a revolutionary movement to correct the problems in our world. It is necessary for each and every voice is to cry out against injustice and wrong. We are witnessing injustice all around us, and we have observed it down through history. Yet changes are happening, too.

"It is a revolution that started a long time ago and continues to this day," he elaborated one evening. "Every person who is a rebel against our democracy is labeled. It doesn't matter if they are protesting our government's exploitation around the world, or its oppression of the poor. They will be criticized and minimized. If you try to help young, lost children, teens, and young adults, you will be rejected, called 'bad for society.'

"The revolution has leaders in every country in every generation," Charlie continued. "They go by different names, but the message is the same, whether they were called Ernesto 'Che' Guevara, Hugo Chavez, Martin Luther King Jr., Malcolm X, Luis Farrakhan, Chairman Mao, Fidel Castro, Pancho Villa, Benito Juarez, or Emiliano Zapata. The list of people goes on and on. The faces are many, but the cause is the same. The establishment has always exploited the poor," he went on, "and thrived off the blood, sweat, and lives of the old and young. The powerful springboard their careers, lacing their pockets with the money better spent to help the poor get a decent education, or help the farmer to modernize his farming equipment. If they choose, they could build better hospitals, schools, houses, roads and bridges. They could clean up our rivers, beaches, air, and soil. Instead, the politicians elected into office do nothing, even though they could make some difference because they have the platform to do so.

"Where the politician has failed, you and I could take a stand." By this time, Charlie was animated and passionate as he preached. I could visualize his arms waving about, punctuating his words and emphasizing the cadence of his ideas. "This, my brothers and sisters, is the medium that I, Charlie Manson, have chosen to use to change the world." I was the only one listening to him, but in his mind he was orating to some large crowd. I don't necessarily agree with every aspect of what Charlie said to me. At the time, I did accept everything he said, unquestioningly. I am now somewhat removed from his words and can think more independently.

Still, I believe that changes are needed. The world will continue to deteriorate until someone does something to grasp our attention. Now I'm not saying that anyone should go blow up a car or building. Rather, I would prefer that everyone take a non-violent stance and utilize the writing of books as a way to reach people all over the world. Inspiring others can be accomplished through music, art, and writing, whatever medium that can be utilized to help spread the word so that it benefits people. Charlie chose art and music. For others, political discussions with their neighbors are probably the fastest, cheapest means of propagating a positive message of change.

Thankfully, today, because of the World Wide Web, it has become possible to help victims all over the world. Those with diseases require medicines and proper care, the poor need food and sustainable jobs, and the orphaned need security and a sense of belonging. All people need the basic building blocks of life and health and purpose. All of us need to help each other, or as Charles Manson would sing on the tier, "Love one another, help your brother." One person at a time, we can make a difference. That is the revolutionary movement that is needed to correct our world's problems.

I would never have understood this if it weren't for my friendship with Charles Manson, and his words reverberate in all areas of my mind: "We are one. There is no you, me, him, they, or them. There is only one!"

Chapter 8
Charlie's Sanity

"I became insane, with long intervals of horrible sanity."
Edgar Allan Poe

Many people ask me whether Charles Manson is insane. My answer is always, "well, yes and no." By the legal definition of sanity, in my presence, Charlie was as sane as you and me. He knows the difference between right and wrong. He was in full awareness of what he was doing and how it was affecting others. In fact, it's this awareness that enables him to act the way he does. He is so sensitive to the actions and thought patterns of others that he is able to manipulate people for his own ends. He studies others to learn their weaknesses, and then uses these weaknesses against them. Acting crazy, and inviting others to conclude that he is in fact crazy, is one way he gets what he wants from other people.

Indeed, many of his actions appeared crazy. They were designed to be this way. He was always very intentional in the moves he made. Charlie did many bizarre things in my presence, and these served to keep others confused and perplexed. Who is the most feared adversary, according to any military strategist? Certainly, it is the insane opponent who may do anything at anytime and whose actions defy rationality. Charlie embraced the identity of the lunatic adversary, and he kept his opponents (and his friends) on edge with a deep sense of unease.

On one occasion, Charlie told another inmate and me to start talking with each other, yelling at the top of our lungs when he said the word, "go." There was no warning, nor prior discussion of this bizarre charade. He simply commanded and expected us to carry out his orders. We didn't know why we should do this or what purpose Charlie had in mind. We also didn't know why we should not participate, so we each for our own reasons decided to comply with Charlie. Perhaps, it was easier to go along with his scheme than to object to it. It might lead to some fun, too. It doesn't take much to amuse an inmate.

When he said, "Go." We began to shout at one another:

"HI, MY NAME IS WILLIE." I could not talk any louder.

"HELLO, BROTHER," yelled Bill. "YOU KNOW WHAT I'D LIKE TO DO?" Bill was talking at the same time as me.

"NO, WHAT?" I asked.

"I'D LIKE TO GO FISHING IN A LARGE LAKE," he screamed. "I WOULD CATCH ME SOME SALMON AND SOME TROUT."

"I'D LIKE TO GO TO MCDONALD'S," I yelled back. "I MISS HAVING A BIG MAC AND FRIES."

"I'M FROM NORTHERN CALIFORNIA," Bill continued. "PEOPLE FROM NORTHERN CALIFORNIA ARE MUCH COOLER THAN–"

Suddenly, Charlie shouted, "STOP." We ceased speaking and sat in silence. Just as suddenly, he got us started once again. Soon, we were laughing like little girls at a slumber party. Crazy? Yes. However, everyone knew who was in control. As usual, the guards were put on notice to expect the unexpected from Charles Manson. Only the newer inmates had questions about what had transpired. The veteran Building Four inmates had seen it all from Charlie before.

At times, Charlie would say crazy things out of the blue. Anyone might think upon hearing about one of these that he must be completely out of touch with reality. As I think about it, however, I realize that he usually had some ulterior motive to say his ridiculous statements. He was entertaining others, he was recapturing control of the conversation, he was putting others on alert with the threat of the unexpected, or he was feigning lunacy to gain sympathy or elude responsibility for something. He may even have used fake insanity as a mask for his insecurities and fears.

He once told me that fish had talked to him while he was at the beach many years ago. I am convinced that he believed what he was saying. I saw no evidence that he was trying to get an untrue story past me. The words of the fish were no life changing pieces of wisdom. They didn't issue commands of the type that a schizophrenic heeds. The words spoken by the fish were no more bizarre, other than their source, than any conversation that happens between friends. Why he felt the need to attribute the words to creatures that swim in the ocean, I couldn't explain, unless, of course, it really happened to him.

The strangest thing he ever said to me was that dead people visit him. "If you want to know what one of your dead relatives has to say, just let me know," he offered. We were talking about something entirely different. I have no idea how his mind wandered to talking with the deceased. "Dead people come to meet me in my cell and sometimes they tell me things about other inmates."

Even in the height of my adoration of Charlie, I was skeptical of these visitors. If it were true that he was visited by the dead, I was certain that my granddad had better things to do beyond the grave than chat with Charlie. I didn't respond to his offer, and he never brought up the subject again.

Charlie did many bizarre things in my presence, things that could be classified as crazy or psychotic. Why he did them is open to debate; that they always put people on edge is not. You could never know what to expect from day to day out of him.

The most heinous action that Charlie carried out was a taunt of the African-Americans on the tier in the most horrible fashion: he dressed as a KKK clansman. It was canteen day when he pulled this stunt. Each inmate prepared himself for his turn to purchase food and toiletries. When it was time for our tier to participate, the inmate whom we called, "Joker," had only a couple of items to purchase. The next inmate had nothing to get so he didn't go to Canteen. I also passed on the opportunity. Then it was Charlie's turn.

Apparently, Charlie had gathered some tee-shirts, cut them to pieces, and sewed the pieces together to create a long, flowing shirt and long, flowing pants. The sleeves of the shirt were flared to look like a clansmen's robe. The pant legs were similarly flared, dragging on the floor. He had taken a pair of state-issue tennis shoes, dyed them black to resemble marching boots or some kind of black biker boots, and put these on to increase the intimidation.

The costume did not contain a pointed hood that would typically accompany such a robe. It was not necessary, however, for others to understand exactly what Charlie was implying. Some weeks later, I did see a small white hood in his cell. It was smaller than what would be expected to match the robe, looking more like a hat worn by one of the seven dwarfs. Perhaps, he goofed in manufacturing it and decided to wear the outfit without the hood.

Donning the unusual garb that could be understood for nothing other than the robe of a clansman on his way to a KKK rally or a lynching, Charlie exited his cell and turned to walk the length of the tier. He didn't turn around to see the reaction that he would inevitably elicit from the other inmates. The tier became very quiet as everyone waited for something to happen.

Upon returning to his cell, and having his lock secured, Charlie turned his attention to the three bags of items he purchased from Canteen. Suddenly, the tier erupted. Someone yelled, "FUCK THE KKK!"

Someone else added, "FUCK CHARLES MANSON." The skin heads upstairs kept quiet. Even they knew that Charlie had shown disrespect in a way that was inexcusable. They wouldn't condone that behavior. They knew that if they had spoken, they would have to be ready for a fight. They had no intention of defending Charlie in that blatant display of threat and intimidation.

What made his behavior so startling was the fact that almost everyone in our section was African-American or part African-American. Our Tier had only three whites, in addition to Charlie, and one white/Indian mix. My friend's home-made outfit could have incited some serious fighting, and the white inmates were overwhelmingly outnumbered.

Charlie had his dark days, but this was by far the darkest I ever saw. I knew that he shouldn't have dressed like that. I am Puerto Rican, black, and Native American. I was offended, but I try to understand where other people are coming from. I don't hate the clan as many people of color do, but I do understand how foolish it is to taunt others for no good reason.

He had previously told me that he had clansmen in his family back in Virginia, though he did not share their sentiments. In fact, Charlie often told me about his efforts to help the "brother." This display on the tier, however, made me question his concern for minorities, particularly African-Americans. Which was it, I pondered. Did he love blacks as he said or did he hate them as he apparently demonstrated? There were many times that I just sat and pondered his actions or his words. Something didn't make sense and I intended to figure it out.

I suspect senility factored into his decision to dress they way he did. He was past his 71st birthday so maybe I should give him a break. Fortunately, nothing came of this demonstration. We were all adults so we let a lot of things go. We couldn't get to each other anyway, if we wanted to make something out of a slight. In general, we let a lot of insults and bad behavior slide on our tier. I like to think that we had a certain level of maturity that allowed us to overlook our differences. Perhaps it was merely convenience that enabled us to ignore each others foibles.

I would forgive Charlie for all the things he did that would make me mad at him. He was old and under a lot of pressure, I knew, and had been through a lot in his life. By that time, he had spent more than eighty percent of his life incarcerated. I knew that I needed to be more understanding of him, and more forgiving. I had too much to work on in my own life to worry about his behavior.

I never saw his clan suit again. I suspect the guards demanded it of him and destroyed it. It was probably removed during the next shakedown, never to be seen again. He never did get written up for it. I suspect because it was too difficult an offense to prosecute: it's hard to interpret a symbol in court, even if the message was very clear on the tier.

In general, Charlie was as good to African-Americans as to anyone else. He was known for his generosity, and the color of an inmate's skin made no difference to him. I saw examples of giving all the time. He gave generously to Hispanics, African-Americans, Asians, and every inmate he thought had a need.

I got to know one particular African-American who was a recipient of his gifts. The inmate on the other side of Charlie, in cell 28, was nicknamed, "Negro." He was an ex-Mexican Mafia member. Tired of the politics, and wanting to focus on his family, he left the gang to become a special-needs inmate like me. We had met previously and were acquaintances of sorts, but being penned near him was a chance for me to get to know him really well. We chatted about Charlie out in the yard one day, away from the old man.

"That Charles Manson is a trip, huh?" I initiated.

"Yeah," Negro replied. "He sure is crazy. I seen Helter Skelter and read a book on him a long time ago. He don't seem to be all that bad. He's cool. Last month, he bought me a bag of coffee and gave me a candy bar. "I've heard about him buying people TVs before." continued Negro.

"Yeah, he has done that," I informed him. "My homeboys told me about that a long time ago." I didn't want to tell Negro that Charlie has promised to give me a television, or that Charlie had given me much, much more than coffee and candy. By that time, Charlie had provided me with a kitchen-sized quantity of food items such as soups, chips, crackers and donuts. My business was mine alone, so to protect my interests, and to protect Charlie from any abuse from this man, I kept silent.

Negro never verbally disrespected Charlie or me, or anyone else that got along with him. However, if someone disrespected him by telling him to, "Shut up," Negro would yell a string of expletives back and bang on the door of his cell for hours at a time. Charlie and I had our own program: we slept when we wanted to, wrote when we wanted do, and did our art when we wanted to. We were usually respectful of others. Negro wasn't. He would stay up late, banging and banging, and then sleep all day to make up for his sleep-deprived state.

Negro carried this out once for four days straight. Charlie and I said nothing. What could we do? Yelling at him would have done no good, but would have added to the noise and confusion. Eventually, the guards had had enough. They sprayed him with mace through the tray slot and rushed him with four large, fully-armored men. They later claimed that Negro was suicidal and had consumed a large number of pills. No one had seen the pills so the story may have been entirely fabricated.

When Charlie still said nothing about Negro, I began to wonder about his commitment to the "brother." He had often advocated for African-Americans in his discussions with me. Now, here was a real example of a brother being mistreated. Was Charlie being disingenuous with me? However, this situation was different, I realized. Negro had created his own waves in the ocean. He was causing the disturbance. He never cleaned his cell and was continually requesting a transfer to the psych unit of a different section. When he banged on his door for four days, he, and he alone, was responsible for the consequences. The guards saw to it that his transfer request was granted.

The very next day, in the quiet of Negro's absence, a guard spoke to me. "Negro was asking for trouble. Don't trip on him and all the trouble he brought on himself." I concluded that the guard was probably right. Perhaps Charlie said nothing because there was no apparent abuse of the man, regardless of the color of his skin. Maybe to Charlie, the color of Negro's skin was irrelevant. Negro acted like a jerk, disrespecting all of us on the tier, and got what was coming to him from the system. I hoped that he came to his senses after his transfer, and that he was doing well in his new home. Maybe, he just needed to find the right place for himself.

One morning when I was sleeping in, I heard noises outside my cell. I heard laughter, keys clinking together, voices, and chains dragging on the cement floor. I got up and went my window to see what was happening. I observed at least fifteen guards of all shapes and sizes pouring onto our tier.

"It's a shakedown," I said to myself. "Damn it!"

I banged on the wall to Charlie's cell to wake him in case he was still sleeping. I ran to my bed, under which I kept my pruno, hidden in a paper bag. I dashed to the toilet as I untied the bag. Tasting the pruno, I noted that some of the sugar was not yet fermented. A few more days and this batch would have been excellent. Still, it had some alcohol in it, and I would be damned if the guards were going to deprive me of all of it.

I took a few sips, as much as I could manage. I banged on Charlie's wall again, "You up, Charlie?"

"Yeah, I've been up all night," was his reply. I guzzled all the pruno I could before pouring the remainder in the toilet. I also flushed my kicker, the pulp that I reused to make batch upon batch of pruno. I wasn't too happy that I would have to start my brewing process all over again, completely from scratch. I had done it often enough after shakedowns, but it was an inordinate amount of work. I knew it would be weeks before my next taste of pruno.

By this time, the force of guards was fully present in the tier. The group fanned out, posting two guards to the front of each cell. "Strip out!" one of the guards assigned to my cell cried. I removed my underwear and deposited it on the floor beside me. I knew the routine.

"Give me your shoes," commanded the other guard posted to my cell. I proceeded to gather my sneakers and pass them to him through the tray slot. Stepping close, the guard looked into my mouth and my ears. He did a quick check of my armpits. There was nothing for him to see. I had never attempted to sequester any contraband on my body. It was a foolhardy risk as inmates were almost always caught. Inmates who tried this inevitably paid a price, legal or otherwise. "Squat and cough," he barked. I complied and allowed him to inspect my privates. "Get dressed and cuff up," he ordered gruffly. There was no discussing with this guard.

I could hear Charlie arguing with the guards assigned to his cell. As I slid my arms through the tray slot in preparation for being cuffed up, I noticed a sergeant and three guards stationed in front of Charlie's door. They were telling him to cooperate so they could complete what they had to do. They informed him that if he didn't obey their commands, they would have to mace him and remove him by force.

Charlie relented as I waited to be cuffed. His guards removed him from his cell and placed him in a temporary cell that was bolted to the floor of the tier. The cage was about ten feet high, constructed of solid steel from top to bottom. It looked to be lightweight for transport, but durable enough to prevent escape. The steel mesh and bars would resist any kick or punch from even the strongest inmate.

All the prisoners from the tier were to be moved to temporary cells on the other side of the building. That is what happened each and every time that there was a shakedown. Our removal enabled the guards to carefully inspect each cell for contraband or escape attempts. Apparently Charlie's defiance had made it necessary for him to be kept on the tier.

Once inside the temporary cell, Charlie began to enact some strange Kung-Fu type of moves. He crouched down, took slow deliberate steps while drawing large arcs with his hands. He resembled a windmill before bringing his hands together and reaching out in the motion of someone plucking an apple from a tree.

"Did you see that?" One guard asked another. "Charlie just grabbed your heart." They laughed out loud. Charlie seemed oblivious to their words. I began to laugh, too. It looked so weird for Charlie to make those menacing moves while completely locked away from everyone else. If anyone wanted to challenge him, they could not. The prisoners were all cuffed up (or about to be cuffed), and the guards were paying him scant attention.

The inmates were all pretty quiet. We had been through many shakedowns before. A couple of men on the tier were asking the guards for gentler treatment. "Don't be trying to disrespect me!" One inmate yelled as he was led away from his cell.

"Just do as you're told and we won't have no problems," replied the guard as he left to corral another inmate. The sun was out; it must have been about seven o'clock in the morning.

When I thought about it later, it occurred to me that Charlie must have requested to be put in the cage. In the course of the shakedown, the rest of us, from ex-gang bangers to special needs inmates, were all taken to cages on the other side of the section. What appeared to be an act of courage and fearlessness was actually a cowardly request covered by false bravado. Evidently, he was so afraid of being moved off the tier that he requested the special privilege of being placed in a temporary holding cell. The guards never let on about his request, allowing him to play the charade of brave and dangerous inmate who needs to be put in a separate cell on the tier. No one but me, to my knowledge, comprehended Charlie's fear in that episode.

Charlie changed his hair style from time to time. This may be a reason that others consider him crazy. He was not interested in current hair styles, fitting in with others, or appealing to anyone's taste but his own. Once, he shaved half his head, leaving the hair on the other half long and flowing. He left his goatee intact. It looked truly bizarre. He explained to me that by attempting to be halfway between good and evil, he could control them both. Jesus had worn long hair, and the devil appears bald in most pictures. By representing them both in his body, he was praising them both.

I told Charlie that he had to choose one or the other. In my mind, you couldn't be both the Satan and God. "There is no in between." I explained to him. "It's one or the other." Charlie disagreed. He wanted to be an abraxas in his own body, a perfect representation of both good and evil, possessing power over them both.

I've since concluded that he is a man of opposites. To describe Charles Manson is to identify conflicting forces. He is the yin and yang, positive and negative. As such, he is just like anyone else, having strengths and weaknesses, but Charlie's attributes are much more pronounced. He possesses both positive and negative forces; he is both good and evil. Those who see him as only evil miss his qualities of caring, of energy, and of love. They will reject him because they say he is such a bad person. Those who see only good are disappointed when they discover that he can show his evil side with no prior notice. In fact, he makes a point of demonstrating evil to provoke fear and shock.

Charlie is a holy man, in many respects, and possesses in his character all the pros and cons that being a holy man entails. He is a flawed human being. As a born leader, he has a way with people, no doubt. He gathers others to himself and sets them on a course of action. In addition, he bears the stresses and strains of being a leader and public figure. He exhibits the shortcomings and weaknesses as all people who are in the public eye. When he does something wrong, it is magnified to far greater proportions than anything I could ever do to mess up. When he does something well, his followers parade it around telling everyone who will listen that Charlie is a savior.

In goodness, Charlie can surpass the humblest Christian martyr. I saw him give and give until it hurt him. I saw him care until it evoked physical pain. Even in the depths of depression, Charlie would look out for the good of others. Yet in weakness, in the cruel place in his heart, Charlie could orchestrate fear, hatred, and even, I believe, death. To deny either part of Charlie's existence does not do justice to such a complicated, complex individual.

Before people criticize, reject, or dismiss Charlie, they need to remember that he thought, felt, drank, ate, slept, and yelled just like you and me. We all must take a long look in the mirror before we throw any stones in his direction.

One event that I witnessed may indeed qualify as an example of Charlie being crazy. He may have lost all sense of reality. To this day,

I don't understand what was taking place or what he was attempting to accomplish. One morning, he requested to take a shower when it was offered. This was a rarity because he greatly preferred to take "bird baths" in the sink of his cell, rather than utilize the community shower. He never accepted an invitation to go to the showers during the scheduled three-times-a-week shower days. This request occurred after yard visit when inmates are also granted the opportunity to go the shower room. I was in shock that the old man agreed to go.

The guard we called "Pinky" got him his towel and unlocked his cell door. Charlie ambled to the shower area. Fifteen minutes later, Charlie returned to his cell fully clothed and dripping wet. It was clear that he had sauntered right into a shower stall and never bothered to remove any of his clothing. He was completely wet; there was not a dry spot on his clothing. His hair was not clean or altered in any way from the way it was when he left his cell. He left a trail of water behind him on the tier as he entered his cell once again. A guard noticed that he had forgotten to bring his soap back from the shower. When Pinky retrieved it for him, he declined to receive it, asking that it be given to me. I could tell that the firm, dry bar had not been used. It was the most bizarre thing I ever saw my friend do. It made his Kung-Fu act in the cage seem relatively normal. To this day, I can only venture a guess at what he was thinking.

Charlie was not crazy, not in my opinion. I got to know him well enough to understand that he was not out of touch with reality. He was not against using what he knew, however, and acting in unconventional ways (truly unconventional) to achieve some end. He was shrewd. He pretended to be insane to keep others in fear of him and to keep others off balance. He knew how to get what he wanted even if it meant strange actions. He was capable of the unexpected, which ironically we all came to expect. Maybe he was crazy like a fox.

Chapter 9
Charlie in Federal Prison at McNeal Island

"The securest place is a prison cell, but there is no liberty."
Benjamin Franklin

Charlie told me that the best school he ever attended was the Federal Prison on McNeal Island. Now converted into a state prison outside of Seattle, Washington, McNeal Island, as it is called, was originally a federal prison. Charlie served time there from 1961 to 1966. He met a variety of characters there, some of whom were able to educate him in areas that would later aid him in understanding and controlling other people.

While at McNeal Island, Charlie became fascinated with hypnotism, he told me. He met an inmate who was an accomplished psychologist who was in prison for tax evasion. Charlie befriended the displaced doctor and asked him about hypnotism. The doctor explained that he used it in his practice to enable others to kick addictive habits and gain control over their lives. Charlie wondered aloud whether hypnotism could be used to control others. The doctor just laughed.

Charlie asked the doctor to teach him how to hypnotize. The doctor agreed. He offered to hypnotize Manson to rid him of his cigarette addiction, as part of the training. This intrigued Manson because, at the time, he was consuming more than two packs of cigarettes on a daily basis. He didn't believe that anyone could do anything that would allow him to quit his stubborn habit.

Charlie was intrigued by how simple the process was, when the doctor finally made time to hypnotize him. The doctor instructed him to look at a circle on a piece of paper, allowing his eyes to trace its perimeter. The doctor then spoke calming words as Charlie moved his eyes slower and slower around the circular shape. The doctor asked him to repeat aloud the following phrases: "I do not smoke," and, "I do not like the taste or smell of tobacco." Charlie spoke the sentences, as commanded, in a slow monotone, almost a drawl, over and over and over. After what seemed like an hour (but was more likely just a few minutes), the doctor "woke" Charlie and engaged him in conversation.

"Would you like a cigarette, Charlie?" the doctor queried.

"No," Manson reflexively replied in a monotone. "I do not smoke. I do not like the smell or taste of tobacco."

After that experience, Charles Manson joined the ranks of the non-smoker, at least for a while. He did not smoke a cigarette for more than a year and didn't feel the desire to return to his former habit. He did crave a deeper understanding of this unusual trance-like state that had such a powerful effect on him and his behavior.

Over the course of several weeks and many discussion sessions, Charlie learned that the human mind was open to suggestion from the self and others when the body is placed into a relaxed state, a far deeper relaxation than is normally achieved in every-day life. Fisherman and lighthouse keepers sometimes achieve something approximating the state while focusing on the repetitive and monotonous motion of the waves. The full state can be induced by artificial means with a trained hypnotist. Charlie never received certification nor took any classes to learn about hypnotism, but came to know as much as many board certified, practicing hypnotherapists.

Charlie also studied Scientology at McNeal Island. A fellow inmate possessed a number of scientology books that he loaned to Charlie. Together, the two of them spent hours discussing the beliefs of L. Ron Hubbard found in the various books. Charlie never expressed a desire to join the movement; he did want to know how it functioned, what its appeal was to so many young people, and how to benefit from its ideas. He told me that he had occasionally introduced himself as a Scientology expert, especially to teenagers in San Francisco in the late 1960s. I suspect that Scientology became one of the staples of his philosophy, something he pulled out of his bag of tricks when needed, whether he told people that he was an expert or not.

Charlie told me about his experiences learning to be a minister. He had met an actual minister at McNeal. This man impressed him, but not nearly as much as his career did. How was it possible for someone to stand up in front of a crowd of people each week to tell them what to think and what to do? Charlie wanted to know.

He befriended the minister in an attempt to learn all he could about the trade. Over time, he queried the clergyman about ministry, about ordination, and about the skills needed to tend a flock. The minister encouraged him in his pursuit, telling him that he had what it took to become a skilled man of God. Throughout their conversations, Charlie feigned an interest in Christianity. The minister thought that Charlie's sincerity and his ability to relate to people would take him through seminary and into a successful career in the pastorate.

They began tutoring sessions. What interested Charlie was not the Bible or any teachings of Christianity, though Charlie picked up many words and phrases that would lead others to believe that he was knowledgeable about the Scriptures. My friend wanted to know how to control others. The power exhibited by a religious leader attracted him like iron filings to a magnet. Charlie demanded to know how religious leaders could direct their followers into all manner of strange practice, from building cathedrals to vowing poverty to fighting crusades. He also wanted to know how he himself could get into a position where he could lead others as they listened to, and venerated, his words.

Charlie told me that what he learned opened his eyes. It isn't knowledge or wisdom that allows someone to gain control over another. It's the character and confidence an individual displays that makes the difference. Even the dimmest of people can attract a following, he had concluded. Classroom attendance and scholarship are not prerequisites. If someone has a message, believes that message deeply, and can inspire others with his words, he can attract a wide following and exert control over the group he builds. While Charlie never said this to me, I suspect that this training was the origins of the Manson family that would later emerge in Northern California, and become known worldwide on December 1, 1969.

Charlie told me that while he was in prison at McNeal, his mother paid him a visit. They sipped lemonade after Charlie ushered his mom into the prison's visitation room. During their discussion, Charlie gave his mother some money and instructed her to purchase a guitar for him. She returned a few weeks later—with no guitar. When asked, she told Charlie that she needed the money for herself and could not afford the guitar for him, even though it was his money. Charlie told me that he was very angry when he walked out on his mother that second visit. He asked to be taken back to his cell, even though he had spent less than 10 minutes with her. At the time, he never wanted to see her again, he told me. He later changed his mind and requested another visit. When she had showed up without a guitar, he had become filled with rage. He hated her. He hated the world. He hated himself. He hated his life. All looked very bleak for Charlie. He was overcome with a bitterness that had first emerged in childhood and was never to leave him.

Charlie noticed a Chinese man performing some strange rituals in the prison yard of McNeal Island. He asked the man what he was doing, to which the man replied that he was a master of Gung Fu, a marshal art. Charlie asked him whether he would be willing to train him in the art and practice of Gung Fu.

It occurred to me that Charlie was adept at noticing the skills of others, and begging for instruction. How many skills had he developed this way, I wondered. He nearly became a bullfighter, he learned hypnotism, and he learned about Scientology. Probably, he picked up additional skills that he never related to me.

"No," was the Chinese man's quick reply. "I don't trust white man. Not trustworthy. They lie."

Charlie was disappointed at the refusal, but not defeated. He set about changing the Gung fu master's mind. For many mornings following that encounter he showed up while the man was conducting his exercises. Striking up a conversation, Charlie learned his name and engaged in small talk. Before long, the man trusted Charlie enough to show him a few moves. The man enjoyed the company of Charlie and began mentoring him in a comprehensive training regimen. Charlie demonstrated a couple of these moves for me, one afternoon. On many other occasions, he struck a carefully balanced pose or made a slow sweeping motion in an effort to impress or intimidate someone.

Charlie also learned some fencing moves while at McNeal Island. One day, an elderly gentleman approached Charlie in the yard.

"May I speak with you?" the man asked.

"What do you want?" Charlie inquired.

"I saw you playing handball in the yard, the other day," the man began. "I saw that you were very quick and could put the ball where you wanted without much effort. I want to show you something, if you have a minute." The man offered.

"Okay, what?" Charlie was interested.

"I used to be a fencing champion at my school," the man continued. "I even competed in the Olympics. I bet that I can put my index finger on your heart no matter what you try to do to stop me."

Charlie was mildly amused, he told me. No old man was quicker than him, he was sure. He knew that he was as quick as the aging athlete that had noticed him on the handball court. Agreeing to the terms of the gentleman's bet, Charlie bent his knees in a ready position and invited the older man to attempt to place his finger on the right side of his chest.

Immediately, the man whipped out his finger and placed in squarely on Charlie's chest, exactly pointing to the heart that was encased in that chest. Charlie did little more than flinch. He was dumbfounded.

"How did you do that?" Charlie demanded to know. "Try that again."

Repeating the process, the old man tapped Charlie on the chest once again with little effort. The younger convict had barely started to block the thrust before the contest was all over. Charlie told me that he became friends with the man, learning about fencing and perfecting some of the moves taught to him. In all of his time at McNeal, he never achieved a quickness that rivaled the old inmate, he confessed. I wondered whether Charlie had in fact been the real initiator with the old man, as he had been with so many other "teachers" in prison. Perhaps, Charlie noticed him and his skill, and not the other way around. No one will likely ever know.

Charlie's time at McNeal Island also helped to shape his perspective on the death penalty. It made no sense to him to purposefully end the life of another human being, not in war and certainly not as the result of some crime. Even the worst of the worse behind bars had talents that could be a benefit to others. Why the state would want to terminate the life of anybody was beyond him. It was also beyond him to understand how putting someone to death would benefit society. No one ever refrained from committing a crime, or changed locations, simply because a particular state had the death penalty while another state did not. Had anyone ever heard of someone lugging an enemy across state lines to put a bullet in his head? Everyone knows that the government has put to death numerous people who were later exonerated, their innocence proven too late to allow any kind of restitution or final justice.

Manson pointed out to me that most people in prison are there because of drug offenses or because of doing something stupid while under the influence of drugs. Charlie always included alcohol when he spoke of drugs. Just because it's legal doesn't make alcohol any less damaging. In fact, more people have killed, stolen, or raped while under the effects of this legal substance than those who have been high on marijuana, cocaine or any other narcotic. Since alcohol remains legal, every other narcotic, all of which had done less damage to people than alcohol, should also be freely available to all citizens. "It might even lead them to a higher consciousness," he observed.

Charlie believed that most people in prison were of a higher quality than the average person not in prison. He convinced me that our judicial system is essentially racist, elitist, and money driven. He had met his share of white collar criminals, even learned from them. What was most noticeable about them, Charlie told me, was the fact that they had shorter prison sentences and eagerly looked forward to returning to their previous lives. Those of lower classes were forever branded for their stay behind bars. Many didn't welcome the uncertainty and the futility of life after confinement, a sentiment most white-collar criminals didn't share.

"Many criminals should be housed in mental institutions," he once related. The prison system isn't a place to reform or treat those who are mentally ill, he was certain. After a few years behind bars, many inmates lose their sanity and need to be treated for depression, suicidal tendencies, or any of a host of other mental illnesses. Others were crazy before sentencing and didn't find proper care in the general population.

Manson convinced me that many inmates are incarcerated simply because they are too good for this world. In carrying out this good nature of theirs, they offered a threat to a society that is lost in its evils. Consequently, many inmates are locked up to prevent them from making society's ills look more egregious than they already do. He never included himself in this category, but I suspect that, if asked, he would say that this was his circumstance too. He repeatedly claimed that he did more good than harm, if he did any harm at all. His good ends were the justification in his mind for some of the acts that ran him afoul of the law.

He pointed to his work with Native Americans as proof that he did much good. Charles Manson is a rare Caucasian who has gained acceptance within the prison's Indian, or Native American, population. Not only did he win friendship and respect from them, he achieved a leadership role among a group of people singularly known for mistrusting outsiders. While he was an inmate at McNeal Island, he gained a reputation for being friendly and charming. He seemed to be able to calm most other inmates and was often called upon by administrators to comfort a prisoner who was out of control. Long before he gained infamy with a reputation for being evil, and developed the accompanying aura of danger, he was generally liked by the inmates and guards.

At McNeal Island, there was one lone Native American. Nicknamed, "Iron Teeth," the large inmate had just physically assaulted his sixth consecutive cell-mate. Because he was so big and muscular, as well as violent, no one wanted to be celled with him, Charlie explained to me. The warden had an insight. Instead of housing this man with an even larger cell-mate, he would try to pair him with Charlie to hopefully produce a positive match. Perhaps Charlie's unthreatening stature and his friendliness would win the day.

Charlie was open to the idea, when approached. His friends told him that he was crazy, but that type of derision had never stopped him in the past. Perhaps Charlie saw the way to an advantage by cooperating with the prison hierarchy; maybe he wanted to get close to this large Native American for some unspecified reason.

As few would have predicted, Manson developed a friend in Iron Teeth. Almost certainly, he used street smarts and charm in lieu of any size or strength advantage. Charlie told the Indian many stories and related to him his own love for, and concern for, the environment. The two men's devotion to Mother Earth drew them close to one another. Over time, other Native Americans were incarcerated at McNeal Island or transferred in from other institutions. No one suggested separating the Manson-Iron Teeth pairing because it was going so well. Manson soon earned the respect of the whole Native American community at McNeal Island. His acts of kindness and his love of nature impressed those who considered themselves at one with the trees and animals. His wisdom was sought by them when issues arose.

When the numbers of the Native Americans housed in the institution had grown to more than twenty, the group chose one of its members to function as a leader, the one who would have the final say in many matters. Leaders were always chosen by the group during a ceremony that involved a sweat lodge, a sort of sauna that functioned as a spiritual experience, a fellowship time, and a formal means of deliberation. For weightier issues, the natives would return to the sweat lodge to discuss and decide. Small issues were always decided by the leader of the band. Minor decisions only rose in prominence if one of the members demanded a gathering, Charlie told me. Through these sweat lodges, members of the various Native American groups represented in prison would cooperate and communicate their needs to one another, later informing the prison's administration of any needs, objections, or frustrations.

One day, it was learned that the current leader would be transferred to a different facility. This greatly upset the community, the members of which would be required to choose a new leader and adjust to the changes. Iron Teeth explained the situation to Charlie and then added a prediction. He told Manson what he had foreseen in a dream: that another Native American would be chosen to be leader, but that a separate role would be created, that of spiritual advisor, a role that Charles Manson would fill. Honored, but more than a little surprised, Charlie made a bet with Iron Teeth that that would not happen. "I've got two packs of smokes and one prison meal that says that you are wrong," Charlie offered. Iron Teeth accepted the bet. Soon after, the large native was called to participate in the sweat lodge.

Just as Iron Teeth had predicted, a new Native American was chosen to lead, and Charlie was invited to be the spiritual advisor of the band.

Charlie accepted the proposal that was unheard of in Native American circles: an outsider invited to join and take a leadership role. The band eagerly welcomed Charlie, granting him the honorary native name, "Walks on Clouds."

Charlie informed me that parole from McNeal Island penitentiary came unexpectedly and quickly. In preparation for life on the outside, he was transferred to Terminal Island Penitentiary, a familiar place where he had served time in the 1950s. Terminal Island, located outside of Los Angeles, functioned as a last prison for many inmates as they transitioned to life after prison. The transfer informed him that he would be released, but it didn't tell him the date of parole. One day, several months into his time at Terminal Island, he was notified that he was to appear before the parole board. With only about an hour's notice, he quickly washed and dressed in his finest attire. He was ushered into a hearing with no wait and with no lawyer. He noted the unusual nature of this meeting and wondered. All his questions were answered when the spokesperson for the board began to speak.

"You have been chosen for parole, Mr. Manson," the man said, reading from a script. "You may gather your belongings. You will be released immediately. Congratulations and good luck!"

This turn of events greatly concerned Charlie. He didn't know how to act on the outside, he told me. Up until then, he had spent nearly half of his life behind bars at one institution or another. The only places he felt truly comfortable, and relatively safe, were highly regulated institutions where he knew the rules and understood the system. He admitted that he was afraid to leave his familiar life behind bars.

He asked the parole board if it was necessary for him to leave, and whether he could stay. To me, his questions appeared more information gathering in nature, and not a plea to remain in prison. The answers he received didn't give him any room to negotiate. The board told him that he had no say in the matter and that he was to be released immediately.

He stepped off the island ferry to freedom on September 11, 1967. He told me that at the time he felt exhilarated but intensely fearful of the future.

Chapter 10
Charlie's Mail and Visitors

"It is strange to be known so universally and yet to be so lonely."
Albert Einstein

I was regularly amazed at the amount of mail Charlie received, something to which I never got accustomed. Several times he informed me that no prisoner in the United States got more mail than him. I don't know how he knew this, but I didn't doubt it, seeing the piles of letters that came his way each day. Usually, he was bragging when he claimed the "postal crown," but once he lamented the volume that had just been delivered. I suspect that he was overwhelmed by his deluge of letters quite often. He couldn't reply to all of the letters he received. Even reading them all would have consumed most of his waking hours.

Every prisoner receives at least some mail. Unpopular inmates only get a letter once or twice a month or less, as well as any inevitable pieces of junk mail; others will receive a small pile each day, especially those inmates who dedicate large portions of their time to preparing missives and responding to numerous pen pals. Charlie, by contrast, practically needed his own postmaster general. On a daily basis, he received stacks and stacks of mail. Everybody, it seemed, wanted a piece of Charlie.

As our friendship blossomed, he would share some of his mail with me. Some of it would make us laugh; other pieces caused us to roll our eyes.

Charlie noted, "Everybody has their angle: this person wants to write a book, that person plans to make a movie." His insights into the schemes of others only reinforced his pessimism toward the human heart. Daily, he had to sort through the avalanche of mail with its demands that came to his cell.

Charlie generally ignored books and magazines. He was not much of a reader. Sometimes, he paged through these to observe the pictures. He might glance at the first paragraph or two of an article that caught his attention, but usually these did not hold much interest for him. He was more interested in the many personal letters he received.

He received so many personal letters that it was all he could do to skim the most interesting ones. Over the course of his many years of incarceration, he had developed a methodical system of moving his mail from an "in pile" to the trash can, a procedure that he worked through almost every day of the year.

Junk mail was quickly identified and deposited in his trash pile. What need he had of credit card offers or home equity loan applications was beyond him. He ridiculed the banks and companies that reached out to him. He didn't need money: he was above and beyond the economy in his mind. "My world is not their world," he declared to me in response to a picture of a flashy boat and a pile of cash.

He saved pieces of blank white paper, heavy stock paper, and cardboard to use in his artwork or his outgoing mail. Rough stock could be used in his art projects for its pulp content. He was generous in sharing the materials that he saved. Our tier never lacked for writing paper, even if it had been torn from the inside of a brochure or was the blank page of a magazine.

Charlie appreciated the magazines and books that were sent to him by friends and concerned admirers, though he never requested them nor agreed to receive them when offered. Depending on the issue, he would skim, discard, or study very carefully what published materials were sent. Very few articles actually held any interest for him. Most of this material was quickly added to the discard pile.

Personal mail received more care. Charlie prioritized it. Letters that were a thinly veiled (or not so thinly veiled) request for something were quickly tossed. Often, he had to read less than a paragraph, sometime only a few words, to realize where the note was headed.

Those letters that came from particular people with whom he corresponded, and those that drew his notice and interest, were given special attention. These were generally set aside until his could dispose of the large volume of mail that proved no attraction. His most personal letters were not shared with anyone, not even with me as we became close. They were evidently for his personal consumption only.

Charlie did share with me many of the letters from people who wanted something from him. Sometimes, he invited me to correspond with these people, if there was something that drew his attention and he thought I might be interested. We regularly shared jokes about the people who made demands of him.

I saw numerous requests that he received from reporters who wanted to write a story or produce a show about him or his crimes. Every time an anniversary of Sharon Tate's murder approached, his volume of requests from newsmen, newswomen, and authors would increase. Some reporters sent questions in their letters. Usually, the queries were neither profound nor original. "Why did you do it?" and "How did you gather your 'family?'" were the most common.

Only a few pieces of his personal mail ever received a reply from Charlie. The letters to which he responded usually came from those who appeared to be part of his inner circle. Whether this was due to the writer's malleability of mind and openness to his ideas, I can only speculate. I knew of no one who engaged in a give and take intellectual discussion with Charlie. Always, it was Charlie's way or the highway. Always.

Charlie passed many of his letters over to my cell. They were good for a chuckle. Not only did people want to sell him things, there were requests for a wide range of items: samples of his pubic hair, pieces of his art, his ideas or opinion some topic or another, his blessing, his advice, or his agreement to live with the sender upon his unlikely parole. Reading his mail was unbelievably entertaining for me. It was clear that Charlie was a celebrity by the amount and type of mail he received. I was honored to be given the opportunity to view hundreds and hundreds of letters and other pieces of mail that Charlie had received.

Reading through the voluminous mail that he shared with me, I was reminded of his words to me. Charlie would often say, "You're going to be famous now!" Being housed beside the old man, I could enjoy what these many people only desired: some attention from Charles Manson. My association with Charlie gave me an insight into the many people who wanted to be close to him.

The letters Charlie disliked the most arrived from Christians. It never made sense to him why sincere people would write him to castigate him for all the bad things he supposedly did, how horrible a person he was, and how he was on his way to hell, only to invite him to join their church. Many, many letters arrived imploring Charlie to repent. Charlie admitted to me that he never felt he had anything of which to repent. He had paid any debt he may have owed to society a long, long time ago by spending so much time in prison. In his opinion, it would be justice for him to be released--the prison system and society owed him an apology. "What about the apology society owes me?" he often lamented.

Charlie also disliked the letters that just told him off. He received his share of this kind of hate mail. On the anniversaries of the Tate and La Bianca murders, in early August, probably spurred by news reports or documentaries, an increased volume of mail arrived from people accusing Charlie of being a serial killer, a baby killer (Sharon Tate was 8 months pregnant), the man responsible for the end of the free and loving 1960s, the one responsible for the killer who terrorized the San Francisco Bay area under the name of "the Zodiac," and any number of other crimes or ills of our society. Charlie got a letter from a man who had spent time in a psychiatric ward. The man wrote to blame Charlie for the mental illness and the institutionalization that the man had received. Though he never met Charlie, apparently he had been attracted to Charlie's image and reputation, and began to model his life after the icon. The letter was sent to criticize and point blame at the man he once venerated and continued to emulate.

Charlie sometimes responded to those who requested his help or offered him something without any strings attached. One writer coveted Charlie's ideas on the topic of change; another sent him some food items without even identifying the sender's last name. Each of these was rewarded with a reply. He was most open to those who sounded sincere, were respectful of him, and were believed to be interesting contacts. Occasionally, Charlie would respond to the kindness of a writer only to find that the gift he had received was sent with some momentous expectations.

Many of the requests he received were blatant grabs for fame and money. One day, he received a check made payable to him in the amount of one dollar. The sender, a man from Texas, invited Manson to, "Use this to get whatever you need." Charlie laughed when he shared this letter with me. It was no secret that the sender hoped to receive Charlie's signature on the cancelled check. "For the price of a dollar plus postage? No way," was Manson's statement to me. I deposited the request in my trash (and not in a bank account) once we were through laughing at it.

Some of the mail was very peculiar. One letter I saw was a request for a donation to a religious organization, a church that worships cows. The letter included a pamphlet detailing how the group was devoted to cows and their protection. It requested donations of $100, $500, or $1000 to preserve the purity of cows. An MIT professor wrote to Charlie, asking him to make a simple line drawing for him. Apparently, the professor was teaching a class on the human mind and wanted to demonstrate the difference between a normal brain with its thought processes, and Charlie's brain. I heard that there is a course being taught at some university on the rap star, Tupac Shakur. Perhaps someone should teach a course on Charles Manson.

Some letters contained offers of assistance. The writers of these letters told Charlie to let them know if he had a need and offered to send money. Charlie would let these individuals know the procedure for mailing items to the prison—along with the rules and regulations that might prevent him from receiving something. Quite frequently, a few weeks later, he would receive food items (purchased through a prison-related company), clothing, tobacco, or even money. Most of these items found there way to other inmates who had need of them.

Many of the offers later turned out to be less than sincere, however. One woman wrote him offering to send him money. Suspicious, Charlie requested that she send $5000. She balked, explaining that she had to take care of her own family before she could help him or anyone else. It was apparent that she never intended to send anything in the first place.

Charlie received plenty of mail from women, some of whom were very willing to help him in any way they could. I do mean, "In any way." I became the recipient of many of these offers when they were passed on to me. One woman from the Ukraine wrote Charlie telling him that she would do anything, absolutely ANYTHING, for him.

"Boxcar, do you want to write a chick from the Ukraine?" Charlie asked me.

"No." I responded. "That's too far away. Shoot me some chicks from the United States, preferably from California or the surrounding states so I can receive visits from them." His piles of mail made my targeted request not as demanding as it might sound. Soon after I said this to Charlie, I was corresponding with dozens of women, all who had first reached out to him. Some were kind and interesting; others were dull or not very friendly. A few of these contacts seemed to be using me, attempting to further a relationship only to get to Charlie. These contacts peppered me with questions about Charlie, what he was doing, what he thought, and how he was coping with life.

More than a few of the letters sent to Charlie were requests for a song or some lyrics. Numerous bands from all over the globe wanted to receive some fresh material from the icon. Some had incorporated Charlie's name, or the name of one of his family members or one of his victims, in the title of their band. Apparently hoping for some legitimacy, they requested endorsements of him.

A few of the letters I read were from individuals claiming to be illegitimate children of Manson's. We both laughed at those. Charlie has been incarcerated in maximum security since 1971, soon after the Tate and LaBianca murders, and these letters came from individuals born in the 1980s and 1990s. We could only wonder what these people were thinking. The sex that Charlie engaged in over that the last forty years wasn't with fertile women! "Dumb asses," Charlie would call them.

Charlie received numerous letters from students. They would send questions for him to aid them in their next term paper or report. He didn't know why he received so many of these: perhaps teachers were suggesting his name, he thought, or the students themselves had a profound interest. Some of the questions from the students that I read included the following: "Why did you do the murders?" "How do you feel being stuck in jail?" "What do you do with your time in prison?" and, "Is it true what is written about you?"

Not infrequently, Charlie received contraband in the mail. Someone would send him a pair of panties, a condom, or a publication that he was not allowed to receive. He would be notified by the prison that the forbidden item had been sent, that it was a violation of law for the prison to forward it on to him, and that, if he chose to, he would have to arrange to have it sent back to the sender. Since it cost him money from his account to have something returned, he usually just ignored the memos.

What Charlie was not able receive in prison included panties, rubbers, bras, cash, food not sent through an approved company, offensive material, drugs (legal or illegal), alcohol, repair tools, heavy equipment, large musical instruments, and books not sent directly from the publisher. All these items would be relegated to a storage room, stacked along side his blue suede shoes, obscene pictures, and paintings deemed to be of a deranged nature. Someday, I expect these items to be made public for all to see and understand a little bit more of the mind of Charles Manson.

Charlie once asked me to respond to a couple of letters for him. I suspect that the pile of letters he wanted to answer had grown so high that he needed the help. He shot me over three letters with his fish line. As I read them, I found that all three were from journalists. One was a request for an interview. Charlie suggested that this woman might be able to supply me with a television and some money for my prison canteen account if I played my cards right. I was honored that he would trust me to speak to the press, given all the stories I had heard from him and all the experiences we had shared by that time. It showed me that even though we bumped heads from time to time, and could get downright nasty with each other, he still saw me as a close associate and trusted confidant.

The second letter was from a producer wanting to create a documentary about Satanism and Satan worship. The letter writer had experienced an exorcism and wanted to tell the world about the reality of demon-possession. The third letter was a request for a television appearance. The producer of a television show hoped to bring cameras into the prison for a one-on-one, sit-down interview with the icon. I responded to all three letters, but not much came of my efforts. Apparently, they all wanted to interact directly with Charlie and couldn't be bothered with me. I never got any money or a television set out of the deal, but I couldn't fault Charlie for trying to help me. He was at least attempting to give me something.

This showed me a side of Charles Manson that few people see, and even fewer understand. If someone wants to sensationalize his life and actions for a television show or a movie of the week, it's not hard to do. It titillates the audience. The truth, however, is much more complex. Charlie, despite whatever crimes he has committed, had a big heart.

Because I generally mistrust others, I was cautious around him at first. I expected and demanded something from him when he requested something of me. In those days, it was quid pro quo in my world. I didn't give anything unless I got something in return. I would ask for cigarettes, money or food items whenever I gave him food items or information about other inmates. Thankfully, he never held it against me. He never demanded anything from, but continued to give generously. As I got to know him, and felt comfortable in our economic dealings, I began to realize that he didn't grasp his possessions as most people do. If someone needed something of his, he was quick to provide. By copying his example, I learned to share as generously (well, nearly as generously) as he did.

When I first started to show him my artwork, he was overjoyed. Like a kid with a new toy, he would really light up to my drawings of animal life. Charlie's heart would melt like butter in an oven if I showed him a scorpion that I had drawn, or if I shared with him a picture of a dolphin or butterfly. He liked my pictures of spiders the most.

At first, he offered to buy some of my artwork with cigarettes or food items. After a few exchanges, where I suspect I got the better of the deal, I began to just give things to him without any expectation of repayment. He even tried to give me things in exchange, but I refused. Soon, we were both giving, heartily and joyfully, and not keeping track of who received what and when.

In addition to the great volume of mail that he received, Charlie had many visitors, more than any other prisoner. A fortunate inmate will get a visit a week from a spouse or close family member. Many get few or none. Charlie's fans nearly beat the doors down to get close to him. Few people were actually granted personal visits, but that didn't stop a parade of reporters, ministers, evangelists, and groupies from requesting to meet him in person. The people who did get to see him were the ones who were already at the prison for some other function. They were the ones who requested and were granted the opportunity to "see" Charlie.

It amazed me to witness the large number of inmates, guards, and prison visitors who clamored to get a glimpse of the icon. Every week, there were people who came to Corcoran to tour the prison facility. They came from junior colleges, universities, and different law enforcement agencies. All these groups visited to learn how the system works, and possibly find employment among the ranks of the Department of Corrections. In addition to these educational visits, some juvenile probation officers brought their charges to participate in a "Scared Straight" program, designed to scare the living hell out of youngsters to steer them away from a life of crime. Part of many visits included a walk past Charles Manson's cell, as a zoo tour would include a trip to the tiger cage. Most participants never approached his cell directly, staying some 30 feet or more away from it as though they could sense danger. They hoped he was not asleep, but if he was, a guard would tap on his window. "Charlie, you've got some visitors," they would say, or "Girl's, Charlie, girls!"

He usually got up to the window and put on a show for the guests. Sometimes, he would wave his arms around mimicking an octopus or he would jump around his cell like a monkey. The visitors usually went away laughing. Once, he put on a fierce expression, and appeared to growl at the spectators. He may have been trying to look like a grizzly bear. Even in his seventies, it was apparent to me that Charlie could still move quickly and be entertaining.

It made Charlie sad that he could have no visits from children. He wasn't allowed any visitors under the age of eighteen. The reasoning behind it really made him angry: because Sharon Tate, one of the victims he was convicted of killing, was eight months pregnant, Charlie had been branded a child killer and deemed to be unsafe around minors. He used to be able to welcome children. Many years ago, he had an adult visit him with several children (I do not recall the facility he was in at the time, if he told me). Since that time, this privilege has been removed from him and he no longer gets to see any children at all.

He told me that in the past, when he had been able to have visitors in a crowded visiting room, many children would come up to him and make friends with him. This undoubtedly occurred before his famous trial on multiple murders. "I couldn't help it if the kids wanted to meet me and play with me," he told me. "Now the authorities have prevented me from being around children. They were just jealous of my popularity!"

During the time I was next to Charlie, he never received a visit from a relative, a friend on the outside, or even a lawyer. Despite the volumes of requests he received, it appeared that few on the outside really cared about him. They may have desired to profit off of his notoriety or possess some evidence of his skill or creativity, but they didn't care about him as a person. I wondered whether his whole life had been like that: was he surrounded by people who took without giving, who profited without providing, and who wanted something without loving in return?

I wondered whether the many letter writers who reached out to Charlie really understood him. Perhaps, they were impressed by his image or the portrait that had been painted of him by the media during the 1960s, and continues to echo to this day. Many of them no doubt thought that they were corresponding with a bearded, charismatic leader in his early 30s. In the backs of their minds, they probably saw the video footage that was shot around the time of his trial and played over and over on television. Everyone wanted something different; no one, it seemed, wanted to know and understand the real Charlie.

Day after day, the piles of mail kept coming.

Chapter 11
The Origins of the Manson Family

"It's like a family"
Unknown female member of the Manson Family

I discussed many topics with Charlie, but by far, the one that most interested me was the murder spree the Manson family undertook in August of 1969. In two nights of mayhem, the Manson family members killed Sharon Tate, those in the house with her, and the LaBiancas, an older couple, the next night in a separate attack. It was these seven murders that led to Charlie's incarceration. They were the most significant events in my friend's life. I decided not to pry to learn the details of what happened, and discover Charlie's role in the murders, if any. I was certain that every prisoner and every guard had questioned him about his involvement in order to gain the truth about the events or to pursue a prurient curiosity. I was sure that he had developed some stock reply to all the questions that arose. I didn't want some fabricated story. I didn't want him to blow me off with some trivial comments. I wanted the truth, so I waited until he himself brought up the topic, and, even then, acted only mildly interested, masking the true depth of my desire to know and understand.

In prison, it's not wise to take too great an interest in someone else's crime. Some curiosity is fine, practically expected. Everyone but the reformed criminal or the inmate who has found religion is eager to

CHARLES MANSON BEHIND BARS

learn new ways of making a quick buck or eluding the police. Convicts learn what not to do by studying how others were caught. Prison, therefore, can be a wonderful educational center to learn all manner of criminal activity. If an inmate is friendly and committed to helping others, he can learn about safe-cracking, armed robbery, burglary, and forgery. Nevertheless, it's best not to act too interested in specific crimes committed by specific inmates. The inmate who asks too many questions looks like a snitch. Since no one likes an inmate who will pass information on to prison guards or to his own lawyer in order to testify against someone, prisoners have to think long and hard before deciding to be a hated snitch. I have seen numerous men beaten to a bloody mess or killed for sharing information about a crime. Even appearing to collect information can be deadly.

I desperately wanted to know if Charlie had committed these murders. I wanted to understand what it felt like to participate in these gruesome crimes, and what it felt like to go through a long trial in the public sphere that was his "trial of the century," long before OJ Simpson captured the public's attention. Charlie was a celebrity and I wanted to participate in his experience. Slowly, the details emerged within our conversations. Too slowly for me at times, but I patiently waited until I understood the story. If there was one commodity I possess in great abundance behind bars, it's the time to be patient.

Charlie never sat down with me and told the story from start to finish. I never expected that and he never offered it. My understanding of the events is a patchwork gleaned from a hundred conversations or parts of conversations. Never once did I bring up the topic of his murders, either. In fact, when he first asked whether I wanted to know some of the details, I declined. Eagerness, I knew, would prevent him from sharing deeply and fully. Instead, I feigned a disinterest that actually served to make Charlie more willing to discuss the events. Probably, he realized that nothing he could tell me could or would be used as a bargaining chip. What judge would agree to reduce my sixty-eight year sentence in exchange for info on Charles Manson, who was already over seventy and who most assuredly never will get out of prison alive? None, we both knew.

The second time he brought up the murders, I just listened. I didn't ask any questions. I didn't comment on what he offered. I think he felt good getting it off his chest. We wove the conversation away from the 1960s many times, but Charlie kept leading conversations back to the events surrounding his murders, and filling me in on additional details.

Charlie had made his way to the Haight-Ashbury neighborhood of San Francisco after being released from Terminal Island prison in 1967, he told me. He had been paroled to the Los Angeles area, but the news out of "the Haight" had been a magnet to the rock-star wannabe. The summer of love called to him and its lure was too great for him to ignore. He wanted to indulge in the free love, drugs, and perpetual party scene. He hoped to build a career as a rock and roll star, and San Francisco appeared to be the place to start construction.

Manson also spent time in Berkeley during the summer of love, 1967. Wanting to participate in the wonderful youth movement that was taking place, he eagerly joined in the communal atmosphere. The environment suited him so well. He told me that he already had an anti-establishment bent as the youth movement was just waking up to the ills of our society. The young people were environmentalists who hated the police and didn't trust politicians anymore. This was so different from the conservative, straight-laced world he left in the 1950s when he was first sent to prison. It seemed that Charlie was a hippie long before the 1960s—the youth culture needed time to catch up to him.

Charlie was welcomed with open arms when he arrived in the San Francisco Bay area, even though he was an ex-con, even though his education was lacking. No one asked very many questions in those days. Everyone in the hippy movement had his or her own story. Few would have guessed that Charlie had spent any time behind bars as he looked and acted no more unusual than the next hippy. Although he was a few years older than most of the hippies, no one seemed to care. The goal of the hippie movement was to be a non-conformist. While some young people labored very hard to capture this ideal, it came naturally to Charlie, his eccentricities, charm and confidence making him popular on the streets.

Northern California proved to be an excellent hunting ground for women. The ones Charlie had prostituted prior to going into prison had departed, never to be seen again. Perhaps they had found other pimps. Perhaps they moved on with their lives. Either way, it did Charlie no good to regret or feel sentimental. He put his mind to the task of gathering new girls. In northern California of the late 1960s, there were many from which to choose. He didn't intend to send women out to the street, initially. In the back of his mind, however, he knew that if push came to shove, that would be an easy way to raise some cash.

Many wayward youth were arriving in California daily. Charlie watched them come in buses and cars. He told me that you could always recognize a new hippie by the disoriented and confused look in her eyes. Maybe they were from the east coast; maybe they were from some small town. Regardless, they were very unsure of themselves and faced with experiences for which life had not prepared them— and it showed. Their clothes were noticeably clean and new, although disheveled in an attempt to make the wearer look rebellious. Charlie laughed out loud when he recounted to me how naïve these girls were.

He worked hard to meet as many people as he could, in those months. He was open to new experiences and new ideas. Mostly, he was open to finding others that would listen to his philosophy and join him in his criminal activities. He looked for girls that bought into the free love atmosphere of the 1960s, ones he could continue to shape and mold. It was a numbers game, he confided in me. Sure, he had difficulty finding a girl and grooming her to trust him in everything. However, the more women he talked to (and he talked to hundreds, if not thousands), the better chance he had of finding one receptive to his teachings and willing to follow him. As his harem grew, so started the Manson family.

Charlie couldn't remember who it was that coined the phrase, "the Manson family," but it was one of his girls, he told me. The girl was talking to a newly-arrived hippy in a park. Manson overheard her invite another girl to join their group. "'It's like a family,'" Charlie quoted her. "'We are the Manson family.'" Charlie liked the name so much that he began to use it. He called the group, "the family," frequently, "the Manson family." He found that a name added to the cohesiveness of the group and gave each of them some ownership. I suspect that he liked it also because it also informed everyone one that he was in charge, in case they were ever tempted to forget. Charlie started his commune with a couple of girls. Soon, others were added, and even a few guys.

Once, Charlie told me that he had to face off against one of the young people that joined his group. A guy named Robert was bothering the girls, pressuring them for sex. None of the girls were interested, and this infuriated Robert. The man started making threats. He told the girls what he would do to them if they didn't agree to sleep with him. He badgered them about how it was an era of free love. One of the girls, fearing that violence might erupt, went to find Charlie.

Charlie told me that he had been very blunt with the man, "Leave the girls alone." He added, "Go find yourself another girl somewhere else. These girls don't want to be with you. Brother, its time for you to leave now!"

Robert left never to be seen again. The girls saw first hand how Charlie would protect them, so they trusted him even more than they already had. They had seen Charlie demonstrate love, and not just talk about it.

Charlie and his burgeoning "family" frequently squatted in unused homes in the early days. His voice cracked with excitement when he recounted to me how many vacant residences there were, and how easy it was to locate one and take it over. There was so much inside each of these places that the family could use or take with them: food, clothing, and even small pieces of furniture. The family tended to trash these houses, stripping them of many possessions before moving on. They tried to enjoy their homesteading while not staying long enough to raise the attention of authorities. The Tate and La Bianca residences were by no means the only homes that were invaded by the Manson family.

Charlie believed that one particular home in which they lived was possessed by evil spirits. It had a painted black line, inside the house, running from the back of the house to its front door. The line appeared to serve no purpose, looking very ugly and visually disruptive, especially compared to the pristine condition of the rest of the home. Charlie told the inhabitants that the line moved power around. They all believed him. The property was owned by a woman who didn't live there, but welcomed people from out of town, giving them a place to crash. There were many young people in and out of the house every day, including many who didn't hang out with his family. One man moved in who spoke very little and had a hatchet tucked into his belt. No one talked with him, sensing that he was either mentally ill or on drugs. After a few days, he was gone like so many other hippies who came and went from the property.

Around that time, while in San Francisco one day, Charlie had an experience that moved him deeply. He was hanging around the docks facing Alcatraz. He wandered through a parking lot, and noticed a small seagull flitting from one discarded candy wrapper to another. He approached a street vendor to purchase three hot dogs and a soda. Still observing the bird, he downed two of the dogs and the drink, and then tossed the last hot dog toward the small gull. Before long, there was a crowd of seagulls, each bird vying for the discarded bun and wiener. Charlie's bird, because it was quick and was the recipient of Manson's generosity, was able to gobble most of his prize and leave only scraps for the others. Charlie noted how the seagull was like him. It was small in a land of giants, yet through pluck and tenacity it was able to get what it needed. It dominated the other birds, despite being diminutive in stature. In the same way, Charlie ruled people in his world, even though he stood just 5 foot 3. In our discussions, it was clear to me that my friend looked for opportunities to compare himself favorably to wild life. In animals, he found friends and fellow strugglers in life. He also found symbols of his experiences.

While in the San Francisco Bay area, Charlie and his girls bought an old school bus. They had collected enough money panhandling and stealing that they could afford the few hundred dollars needed for the bus and a full gas tank. They used their new wheels to travel the west coast. They looked for others to join them, often picking up hitchhikers, and talking to anyone they met. Some of their new friends just wanted a ride somewhere, others stayed with the group a few days. A few became full-time family members as the group continued to grow.

Charlie became disillusioned with the Haight-Ashbury district in 1968. What had started out with the great ideals of love and sharing was eventually becoming little more than a haven for squalor and drug abuse. Many of the original hippies had moved on to new areas or new challenges, some returning to their civilian lives with jobs and responsibilities. The hippies who remained in San Francisco were more recent run-aways or those whose drug abuse forced them to remain on the streets. The magic was gone so Charlie left too.

Charlie and his girls traveled as far north as Washington State and as far south as San Diego and a couple hundred miles into Mexico. They kept returning to Hollywood because Manson liked that area so much. "The weather is perfect there," he told me. "It's no wonder that movie stars and famous musicians end up there." He also hoped to break into the music business in southern California.

An important theme to Charlie, I could tell, was the control of people. Charlie regularly told me how he managed the actions of others and how it was crucial for success to be able to manipulate other people. He told me that there is a great misconception about leading others. So many people think that to make others do what you want them to do means that you must boss them around, telling them what to do and how to do it. Charlie disagreed with this philosophy. He hated following orders and knew that most other people did too. "To control other people," he told me, "you have to let them do what they want to do." He acknowledged the contradiction, but said it was true: "If you want people to follow you, you have to let them do what they want to do. If you let others be free, they'll follow you wherever you fly. You just gotta let them be free."

I wondered whether this Zen-like wisdom was true. It would seem that if you let others be free and do whatever they wanted, they would desire to not follow. I thought following was the exact opposite of being free. Don't people seek to be free from following? Charlie had found exactly the opposite to be true. Perhaps there was something else that Charlie did, or was, that attracted so many people. There must be something to his charm that enabled him to send young women out to the street to earn him money. There must have been something to his personality that attracted others to join his family.

He was adamant about the need for control within the "family." He told me that everyone was allowed to stay with him and his group. There were no exceptions; everyone was welcome. However, as I learned in subsequent conversations, everyone was also told not to cause trouble. If anyone did, the welcome quickly faded. Sometimes, Charlie had to threaten members who were getting out of line. Charlie warned more than a few people that they would become "closer to the earth" if they did not change their ways. Once, a dog was acting weird and not leaving people alone. It became so annoying (and not in a cute way) that Charlie got up, grabbed his gun, and took the mutt for a walk. It was never seen again. The man who usually stuck up for the animals didn't tell me what happened to the dog. He didn't have to. Apparently, not all animals received tender care from Charles Manson.

Charlie was adversely affected by drug use in the 1960s. He told me that he often took marijuana, which was much weaker in the late 1960s than marijuana is today. He was also a regular LSD user. Most of his acid trips went without incident, but he did have a few trips that really scared him. He slugged a couple of women during one trip, and was quite ashamed of it. He used cocaine when it was available and even experimented with heroine, though he didn't like the effect that heroine gave him. He got high a few times with mescaline and some other hallucinogens.

During his time in Berkeley, he consumed drugs daily, frequently mixing several different ones together. Alcohol was also a constant in his life at this time. Of all the drugs and alcohol that he consumed on the outside, he confided to me that he missed the taste of cold beer. Drugs were available to him behind bars. Even inmate-created alcohol is omnipresent. For Charlie, none of these compare to the experience of drinking a pitcher of ice-cold beer in a bar full of friendly and rowdy patrons.

While Charlie took advantage of people during his time of freedom in California, he also helped a great many as well. He was generous to anyone in need. One woman who Charlie helped was affectionately named, "Yellow." When he met her, she was pregnant with only days left in her pregnancy. She was scared and alone. She didn't know what to do, returning home not being an option. Charlie gave her the first positive attention she had ever received. She was grateful that Charlie allowed her to hang out with him and his friends.

When she went into labor, Charlie was there ordering others to get towels and warm water. He cleaned her genitals to prepare for the baby's arrival. He gently steered the baby's head as it emerged into the world. Charlie told me that he was as proud to cut the baby's umbilical cord as if it had been his own child. Yellow named the boy, "Elf." After a few months, mother and child departed from the group. A couple decades later, Charlie received a letter from Elf and continued to correspond with him for many years.

Charlie told me that around that time, he frequented bars. He would visit with his guitar and play for others. Occasionally, he found resistance and ridicule from redneck types. This didn't deter him. If necessary, he fought for his right to party. The bar scene included many drugs, regular fights, and lots of women. Sometimes, he would be invited to join a private party at someone's home.

At one of these parties, he met Dennis Wilson who had achieved fame as a member of the rock and roll band, the Beach Boys. Dennis had also given a ride to a couple of Manson's girls when they were hitchhiking. After listening to Charlie for a while, Dennis expressed an interest in his music. "Take all you want," offered Manson. This was typical of his attitude. In the free love and sharing environment of the 1960s, he knew that if he gave generously, he would never have to worry about not receiving generously. Too, he was not into material wealth. He preached a gospel of love, distaining greed in all its forms. He expected Dennis to remember him later on, if his new friend benefited from the gifts that were bestowed on him. Charlie moved into Dennis' mansion with the girls. It was a great arrangement for Charlie, at least until things soured.

Dennis asked the group to leave after a few weeks, apparently dismayed by the family's disinterest in work and their unwillingness to contributing anything for their room and board. The free ride was over. The family had been living off Dennis, and they all knew it.

Soon, Wilson began to socialize in circles that didn't include Charlie. He lived in a world of glamour and wealth with other celebrities. He had massive riches, but was equally awash in debt. As easily as any of the Beach Boy's, Dennis could go into a car dealership or jewelry store and walk out with his choice of items, leaving only a signature behind as collateral.

Several months later, according to Charlie, Dennis attended a party to which Charlie has also been invited. Without so much as a word, the famous musician, remembering the songs he had received from Charlie, gave the song-writer a brand new Ferrari. Dennis never said a word, just handed Charlie the keys and walked away. Because Charlie didn't care for riches, he showed himself to be one of the most generous people who ever lived by giving his new car away to someone who "needed a ride." He never heard what happened to that car or to its recipient. Probably never before, or since, has a sports car changed so many hands so quickly.

Charlie told me that in Los Angeles, he found a cape in a clothing store. It was black on the outside with a red lining, Charlie's two favorite colors. It looked like a movie prop from a production of Dracula. Charlie purchased it and proceeded to wear it every day. He thought it made him look dignified, like some kind of mafia don. His girls liked it, too. He got a lot of looks as he walked down the streets of Los Angeles. The attention he drew to himself included many long looks from police officers gliding down the street in their patrol cars. Not wanting that kind of publicity, he got rid of the cape after a few days. Charlie seemed to get into the strangest of situations, I noted. I wondered if that was by choice because he went looking for them, by luck for he was always in the wrong place at the wrong time, or by character, proving that weird things happen to weird people. I suspected that it was a combination of all three.

Charlie told me that he was once threatened by man pointing a gun at him. Charlie had been sending some women out to gather discarded food or make a quick buck with drugs on the streets of Los Angeles. One drug customer, a young man named Martin, ran away from one of his girls after refusing to pay. He had previously beaten another of Manson's girls. Charlie decided not to take any disrespect and caught up with the man in an alley behind a bar they frequented.

Upon seeing Manson, Martin pulled out a 9mm pistol and pointed it at him, though he didn't appear willing to use it, Charlie told me. Charlie ran up to him, hit he gun out of his way and pounded on the man's face. Martin was left in a pool of blood, lying in the alley, absent his gun.

I think Charlie told me this story to impress upon me the need to be strong. "If your gonna pull a gun out," he warned, "you had better be prepared to use it. Otherwise, don't bother carrying it." He also wanted me to know that he was not afraid of anyone or anything, not even a weapon. "You can't let people treat you with disrespect," he added. "You have to stand up to them or else they will walk all over you every time."

Charlie told me that he went to Death Valley on numerous occasions during this time. He was fascinated by the name and the mystique of living in a desert. Though he had no personal connection to the area, he met a variety of interesting characters there, including Whiskey Jim who could walk in the desert for hours while sipping water from whiskey bottles.

Charlie explained to me that while in Death Valley, he learned about the burrowing owl, a particular breed of owl well suited to live in the hot sun. To escape the heat, it would burrow into the sand or into any dirt that it could find. Charlie told me that he identified with the bird. He saw it as a kindred spirit: he was in Death Valley to avoid the heat too, only his heat was the attention he received from the police and modern society whose values he could not understand or accept.

In Los Angeles, Charlie continued to collect people he termed, "throw aways." He called them, "throw-aways," because no one wanted these drifters. They were an eyesore to most people, and a threat to the establishment. They were dirty, smelly, and hungry. These were the daughters and sons who had run away from impressive homes and respectable parents in a quest to find something more interesting or more meaningful in life. Charlie wondered what was so bad about their lives that made them migrate to California. He himself had never experienced a stable home, and concluded that their lives had not been all that stable either.

Charlie told me that he was the only one who would care for these people. Grateful for a helping hand and a friend, some individuals began to associate with Charlie and travel around with him. The women would do anything for him, none short of illegal drug dealing and prostitution. The men often hung around for the sex that Charlie could grant them from the girls. They too were put to use dealing drugs. A couple of gay guys among the family members agreed to homosexual prostitution, yet another avenue of income for Charlie.

At the time of the murders, Charlie's "family" had grown to about thirty people, mostly girls with a handful of guys. They resided at the Spahn movie ranch. They crashed at several buildings, including a trailer that was formerly used by Ronald Reagan during his movie-making days. The murders, Charlie confided, occurred on evening missions from the Spahn ranch.

Charlie remained bitter over the two incidences that resulted in his incarceration. He insisted that he was innocent of all wrong doing in those murders. He was not in the houses and had instructed no one to do anything nefarious at all. "I didn't kill nobody," Charlie regularly repeated. The police had pressured some of the people involved to finger Charlie in exchange for a reduced sentence. Linda Kasabian agreed to testify against Charlie in exchange for complete immunity from prosecution. She participated in both murder scenes, Charlie told me. Her hands were covered in blood, both figuratively and literally. "How could she be trusted?" Charlie ranted. "She just testified to save her own ass. She told lie after lie. She told them what they told her to tell them."

Charlie told me that he heard nothing about the Tate murders until after the events had occurred. He suspected that it was a robbery gone wrong. "I think the girls were there to find food and cash," Charlie speculated. "They were pretty deep into drugs at that time. I tried to get them to cool it with the hard stuff."

He also postulated another theory. "They may have been trying to cover up a previous murder," Charlie added. "Our friend Bobby Beausoleil had killed a guy named Gary Hinman. Some words were written in blood on the walls of Gary's apartment. The girls may have figured that if they committed a crime and wrote things on the walls, the police might have concluded that the murderer was still on the loose, and Bobby may have been released from prison. I think the girls went to steal, but somehow things got out of hand."

"Probably, the large number of people in the house scared them," Charlie guessed. "Maybe, someone put up a fight." Five dead bodies were found on August 9, 1969, the morning after the attack. Sharon Tate, wife of film director Roman Polanski, several friends of hers, and a teenager who had been in the wrong place at the wrong time, had each been butchered with a knife, shot, or hung with rope. Some were attacked with more than one weapon.

Charlie claimed that the unborn baby was cut out of Sharon Tate and eaten. He never said who did the cutting or who did the eating. I heard from news reports that Charlie was not in the house at the time. Charlie once hinted that the investigators got it wrong, that he had been to the home where the killing took place, though he never committed any of the murders. I cannot imagine Charlie as the one who killed Sharon Tate, or the one who ate her fetus. I'm not sure what to think of him claiming not to have been in the house, then suggesting that he had been. Maybe he was testing my reaction.

"I went with the group the next night." Charlie told me. "We were looking for food and cash. That's all we ever took. It's not like we meant to hurt anyone. We just wanted the rich people to share what they had, just as we shared with each other in northern California. When I was done tying the couple up, and taking the food we needed, I returned to the car.

"I have no idea why the girls killed those two," Charlie claimed. "They never did anything to us. We didn't even know them. I think the girls were just plain crazy. They were intending to write on the walls. That's it. There was no plan for murder. I got blamed because they were younger than me." Charlie sounded like an accused older sibling who was wrongly implicated in the disobedient act of a younger brother or sister.

Charlie was charged with murder and demonized as the leader of the kids. He told me that he resented being blamed for what others did. "I never told nobody to do nothing." He proclaimed. "I gave them freedom. I let them be whoever they wanted to be. I let them do whatever they wanted to do, and this is how I got treated."

At this point in the conversation, Charlie compared himself to Christ, explaining that just as Jesus was popular among the needy for helping them, and ended up dead, so he was reviled for his caring and his popularity, and given the metaphoric death of imprisonment. I asked him whether he thought he was Jesus. He replied by telling me that what he thought did not matter. What mattered was the truth. He confided in me that he was Jesus, the devil, God, the Buddha, or anything else people wanted him to be. Often, he pointed out that Jesus called himself the "Son of Man," making it clear to me that "Manson" and "the son of man" were interchangeable to him, even if he didn't come right out and say it.

I asked Charlie, one day when we were having a heart-to-heart conversation, whether he in fact ordered the killings that were committed by the Manson Family. He replied, "I didn't have to." When I asked him to clarify, he explained to me that leaders are able to insulate themselves from blame for what their underlings do. He pointed out that American presidents regularly claim that they didn't order this or that illegal activity, even though they had full knowledge of what was going to take place. A president's advisors will take the fall, if criminal activity is ever discovered. Charlie claimed similar executive privilege for himself.

"So you knew about the killings and let them happen even if you didn't order them?" I asked.

"All I'm saying is that I didn't have to order nothing." Charlie changed the topic and would not answer any more of my questions on the topic.

If Charlie were to be retried on the charges that got him sent to prison, I have no doubt that he would be acquitted and set free. I am not a member of the California State Bar Association, but the information that Charlie related to me proves to me that he would walk out of court a free man. Not only liberated, he would likely receive a large settlement check from the state of California.

Tex Watson, one of Manson's most trusted "family" members had testified against Charlie in return for a reduced sentence. Tex told the court that Charlie had been the mastermind behind all the killings, the one in control of the events. However, that's not good evidence against Charlie. Tex couldn't be believed because he had a vested interest in making up a story. To escape greater punishment, Tex would have told the court anything that the prosecutors asked him to say, anything at all.

Charlie told me that he hadn't been allowed to call any witnesses in his own defense. Time and time again, he asked the judge for permission to represent himself in court. Each time he was denied. His defense lawyer didn't represent him well: he didn't allow Charlie to testify to his side of the story, and didn't call a single witness in Charlie's defense. All this would come out in a retrial or in an unbiased appeal.

Charlie has tried to prove his innocence, but without success. One lawyer, many years ago, offered to help him overturn his conviction. Instead of aiding Charlie, the unscrupulous man gathered all the information that Charlie could supply him with, and wrote a book. He had no intention of helping get Charlie free. His work of defaming Charlie probably made it more difficult for Charlie to get a fair trial and get out of prison.

My friend said to me with sadness in his voice, "Boxcar, it's better to just stay in here than to put all my hope into a lawyer who may not give his all to get me out."

I asked whether the bar association could disbar the deceitful lawyer for his lack of ethics and the disservice he provided. Charlie responded that the lawyer in question had taken his millions of dollars from the book and fled the country. "He could've helped me," he moaned. "Instead, he took the money and ran."

Charlie hated the way the media portrayed him. "All they show is footage of me being walked to court," he complained, "then they show the girls crawling along the sidewalk. That's not who I am. Those girls did what they did to demonstrate against injustice. ALL INJUSTICE. That wasn't just about me!"

Every anniversary of the death of Sharon Tate, Manson gets featured in a television show about the murder spree that killed seven people. Charlie hates these shows because he thinks they give a distorted picture of him. When thoroughly frustrated with the world and his mistreatment, Charlie turned to his music and his art for solace. In the most difficult of times, art and music were his only solace.

Chapter 12
Charlie's Art and Music

"Music expresses that which cannot be said and on which
it is impossible to be silent."
Victor Hugo

As I got to know Charlie, I came to see him as one of the most talented people I had ever known—in prison or beyond the walls. He demonstrated skill in music, in creativity, in art, and in lyrics. I began to wonder if there was an area in which he was not gifted. He was no prodigy, to be sure. I never saw him do a parlor trick with his talents, but he was able to master so much of life behind bars. While many inmates wondered what to do to fill their time, Charlie always seemed to be busy as he pursued his many interests.

Music was by far his greatest love. Charlie once told me that he could take anyone and very quickly teach him how to sing. "He would be the perfect singer in 15 minutes," he boasted. I assumed he was referring to voice coaching and hypnosis. Since it never appealed to me, I never took him up on the offer. I was curious, and now regret not asking more questions. At the time, I was doubtful of his claims. Perhaps he could teach a child to carry a tune, I concluded, but not much else. I'm not so sure anymore.

As we talked about music, Charlie shared with me some of the songs that he enjoyed. Because his music was before my time, he had to tell me about Frank Sinatra, fats Domino, and so many other musicians. The oldest band of which I had any familiarity was the Beatles, who broke up when I was a toddler. I asked whether the murders he was charged with were inspired by that British group's music.

He denied it. "The prosecutor invented the story that I killed in response to so-called messages in the Beatles songs," Manson assured me. "The girls had written phrases from Beatles songs on the walls in blood because those were the words that they liked best. They thought that they were common words so that they could never be traced back to them." Stupidly, they had also written similar words on the walls of Spahn Ranch, though not in blood. Charlie told me that he liked most of the songs written and performed by the Fab Four. "That had nothing to do with who I am and what I'm about," he informed me. "I did play music and sing at Spahn Ranch, but my music was about love and about caring."

Charlie shared his artwork with me as he came to trust me. I was astounded by the things he was able to do. He demonstrated a talent and resourcefulness I was not aware even existed. To do what he was able to do would have been difficult for any artist on the outside with all the materials within reach. Charlie expressed his creativity not only in his art, but also in his ability to take the limited amount of prison supplies and use them as though he had a full art studio.

He showed me some beads that he had fashioned entirely out of bathroom tissue. He taught me how to make them, as well. "All you need to do," he explained, "is get a sheet of toilet paper, fold it lengthwise, and wrap it around the insert of a pen. As it is being set in place, the paper needs to be wetted. When it is fully wrapped about the pen insert, you take string and wind it tightly about the paper, using a crisscross pattern. As the string is pulled tight, the water will get squeezed out of the toilet paper. By loosening and rewrapping the string around the paper, the donut shaped mass gets harder and harder." I found that with a little patience and practice, I could make a bead that dried to a density of rock or hard plastic.

Charlie explained out that once the water is squeezed out of the paper "donut," the paper has to be carefully slid off the pen insert so that the drying process can be completed. When several hours, preferably days, have elapsed, the bead, I learned, can be painted with a mixture of

Kool-Aid powder and water, ink from the pen insert, or whatever other coloring is available. It is best to do the painting in stages so that the paper does not get soggy and come apart. Larger beads can be created with two or even three sheets of bathroom tissue used at a time. The beads that he created, and showed me, were unbelievably hard, harder than any wooden bead I had ever felt. If someone didn't know, he or she would never have guessed that the beads were created out of toilet paper and not a hardwood plank.

The development of a painting utensil requires no less creativity. A tiny paint brush can be constructed out of strands of hair forced into another pen insert. Charlie described the process as I listened intently. I now know that if you stuff the pen insert with a wad of moist paper, once a few strands of hair have been threaded into the insert, you can create a rather durable brush. The shorter the hair that protrudes from the brush, the more detailed the artwork that can be managed.

Once several beads were produced, they could be displayed together on a string or rope. Charlie showed me how to make the rope too, which can be fashioned out of the elastic band of boxer shorts. If you carefully peel layers of the band from around the tops of typical shorts, you can soon amass great lengths of stretchy material, even from a single pair of underwear. These rubber filaments can be braided together or wrapped around a pen insert in several directions. By repeating the braiding into larger and larger thicknesses, or providing more and more layers on the pen insert, you can make the rope as thick as you like. Inmates have committed suicide by hanging themselves with this type of woven strand. Consequently, prisons don't allow inmates who are on suicide watch to be left alone in their cells, unobserved, lest they manufacture this or some other type of homemade device.

Beads and rope can be assembled into bracelets, anklets, or necklaces. Anyone can produce the jewelry in the exact same manner as was done by Charles Manson, but few have the patience to make them as intricately and accurately as he did. I suspect that many of his tricks were taught to him by other inmates, just as he graciously shared the things that he knew with me and anyone else who cared to learn. Charlie provided me with many samples of his work and lots of advice in how to perfect my artistic creations. He warned me, though, to keep the pieces well hidden. Some of them are contraband and could lead authorities directly back to him.

Charlie informed me that there is a room in the prison full of contraband items taken from inmates. He boasted that there was a separate room containing only the stuff that had been taken from him: oil paintings, jewelry, drawings, as well as items sent to him from well-meaning fans, such as shoes, pants, shirts, hats, harps, and water colors. I believed him because I saw many items removed from his cell during repeated shakedowns. It became a sort of cat and mouse game between Charlie and his guards: Charlie attempting to conceal items and the guards determined to find them. Generally, these confiscations were done respectfully, each side acknowledging the others' ability and need to compete.

On one particular shakedown, I did lose some of the things Charlie had entrusted to me. I was so angry. He had shown faith in me, and I had repaid it by allowing the guards to find and take Charlie's things. I lost about six beads and two larger pieces of art, a painting of a scorpion and a drawing of a mutilated woman. I would be more careful in the future with the things given to me by my friend, I resolved. I apologized profusely to Charlie. He assured me that it was no big deal.

Charlie had told me about his "Satan's Babies," his hand-crafted spiders, but for many months, I never saw one. One day, he ordered me to shoot him my fishing line over because he wanted to show me something. I gathered my line and caste my car in the direction of his cell. In one smooth motion, the car swung around the cinder block wall that separated our cells, and landed with a thump within his reach.

Charlie drew in some of the slack that remained. After tying something to my line, he jerked it tight. "OK pull, Soul. Pull it slowly," he demanded.

When my car was fully back in my cell, I found one of Charlie's works of art tied to it. It was a large spider, a Satan's Baby, about the size of my hand. It was an amazing representation of a real arachnid with the detail of authentic legs and tiny body hairs. It was entirely white, however, as though it had been born albino. I found it hard to believe that it could have been created behind bars.

"Wow, Charlie! It looks so real," I told him. "It looks like a real spider." I was not trying to impress him or gain favor with my words. I was truly amazed at what I was holding.

"Soul, it took me 30 years to perfect how to make them," Charlie bragged. He pointed out some of the detail that had eluded me, as though it were a real child, his baby.

"Hey, Charlie, are you going to color it," I inquired.

"Boxcar, paint it for me, will you?" His words were halfway between a request and a command. I knew that just holding his artwork was a real honor for me, one that he would grant to precious few people. How much did he trust me and care for me to allow me to paint his creation, I wondered.

"Sure, I could color it with ink from a black ball point pen," I offered.

"That's cool with me," assured Charlie. I grinned with pride that he was open to my suggestion. I inspected the spider again to assure myself that this was not merely a piece made in error, one that he was casting off in my direction rather than throwing it in the trash. I was pleased to see that the spider was perfect in every detail. This was no error; this was the work of a master.

I set about painting it immediately, completing the task in about forty five minutes. Because the spider needed about two hours to dry, I carefully placed it in a used potato chip bag that had been wiped and rinsed to the sterility of a surgeon's scalpel.

"Hey Soul, I'm finished with it," I informed Charlie later that day, "but it needs to dry. Soul, put it somewhere out of the way to dry, okay?"

"Boxcar, you are done coloring it already?" Charlie was surprised. Apparently, he didn't realize how important this task was to me. I had done it quickly, but as carefully as if it were to be displayed in the Louvre.

"Yeah, Charlie," I responded. "I did it just like you wanted. Now it looks like a real, live spider."

"That's good, Boxcar. That was really fast." Charlie's appreciation was clear. He slowly pulled his fishing line toward his cell, tenderly receiving the chip bag once it was within his grasp.

"Do you have enough string left to make me a scorpion?" I asked. I recalled Charlie offering to make me one several weeks prior. Charlie laughed.

"I got enough to make you a scorpion," Charlie answered. "Soul, it's just a little time from my sentence. The only thing that gets in the way is getting an extra pairs of boxers."

"I know what you mean, Charlie," I empathized, "but it's a lot of work too, and I appreciate it." I hoped that my gratitude appeared as sincere as I experienced it. I was certain that my friend had heard all kinds of false statements of appreciation from his fawning fans who wanted something from him. I wasn't looking to receive from him; I was honored to receive what I had gotten already, which was much more than I deserved.

"Yes, but I've been doing this for so many years now that it's easy for me to do." Charlie countered, "I've gotten better and better at it. Nobody can make these babies as good or as fast as me.

"I've got a doll in Japan at the House of the Dead," he continued. "The only way you can get a doll displayed in that museum is to be dead. Well, I'm a dead man walking three times so they put my doll in there. It's a two-foot high doll. The ties on it are really small, too."

"I bet its worth a lot of money," I offered. Charlie went silent as he set about his next task. I hoped that he was working on the scorpion for me.

Charlie also created melodious harps. He once offered to show me one and even make one for me one. "You can tune it and play it like a real harp," he had explained.

The next day, Charlie called over to me: "Boxcar, shoot me your line. I've got something for you. Shoot me a chip bag, too."

I rushed to get a chip bag and line ready to extend to Charlie. I was eager to talk with him, but my curiosity consumed me. What was my friend going to show me this time? When he had my line in his possession, he told me to pull back slowly. I found one of Charlie's scorpions in the bag when it finally arrived back in my cell. I was in awe. It was more intricate and delicate than the spider I had just painted for him. I couldn't image how he created it in less than twenty-four hours. Perhaps he had started, or even completed it, weeks ago, I considered.

"Charlie, I'm going to color it black," I promised. I was feeling very emotional at this gift. No one had given me anything like this before.

"Boxcar, a black scorpion is the most deadly scorpion in the whole wide world," he told me. "It's called the Emperor Scorpion."

"Is that right?" I didn't doubt his knowledge of animals, particularly deadly ones.

"Yes, one sting from an Emperor Scorpion and you're dead real fast," he warned.

I thanked Charlie, but he didn't like me showing appreciation. "Boxcar, don't tell me, 'thank you.'" His words became strangely serious. "Hobos don't have to say 'thank you' because they get what they got coming, so there's no need to say it to me, Soul. Understand?"

"Yeah, I understand, Charlie." I didn't understand what he was talking about. I did understand that I was not to thank him for his generosity. Whether he blurted this out in a need for control or out of embarrassment, I don't know. I made a mental note not to say "thank you" to him ever again. I would have to find alternate ways to express my appreciation for him, I realized.

About two weeks later, soon after I had colored the scorpion to a menacing purple-black shade, I began to hear a strange sound emanating from Charlie's cell.

"Boing, boing, boing." It sounded like the twanging of a door stop or the reverberations of a flexible strip of metal slapped against on the top of a table.

"Boxcar, can you hear this?" Charlie asked me. There was no question that everyone on the tier could hear it.

"Yeah, I can hear it." I replied. How was it possible to not hear it, unless you were approaching complete deafness, I wondered. It appeared as though Charlie was trying to get my attention, rather than the usual other way around. "What is it?" I asked.

"It's a string on a harp I've made, "Charlie gloated. "I'm tuning it right now." The delight in his voice was contagious. "When you come out for shower, take a look in my cell. That way I can keep it out of sight of the guards."

We had showers at 2:15 that afternoon. I was third on our tier to make the trek to the shower room. I peeked into Charlie's window as I walked past his cell. I tried to do it smoothly so as not to draw unnecessary attention to myself or to Charlie's harp. Several inmates had been written up for disrupting the tier while heading to the shower. I didn't intend to join that group. I caste a glance into his cell and saw his harp. He was holding it up toward the window as if he were offering it for auction. He was proud of it, and I was honored to see it.

It was truly an amazing piece of art—and it played too! I wondered how many hours had been used to fashion it and what Charlie had used to create it.

"Hey, Charlie," I said after I had returned to my cell. "That's a trip. You actually made a harp that plays. I can't believe it."

"I told you, Soul," Charlie said, "I've been doing this for years and years. Did you see the beads on it to separate the strings?"

"Yes, I saw them." I had also seen that they were black.

By this time, all the strings were in place and Charlie was attempting to tune them. They each made a distinct sound that promised to harmonize in a soothing melody once they were all accurately tightened. This was the most creative item I had ever seen fashioned in a cell. Charlie told me that it was made solely of toilet paper, dental floss, and some elastic from boxer shorts. Other, mostly food, items were used to color it. For this creation alone, Charles Manson could be considered a genius. However, I saw more, far, far more emanating from this man's brain.

I asked him how he made the harp, one day. I actually had to ask him a second time because he was not facing the right direction when I spoke or his hearing was causing him problems again.

"Well, Boxcar," Charlie began. "How I make a harp is to get piles of toilet paper arranged on my sink. I get so many piles that I can wet them and arrange them around the rim of my sink. I've also used the toilet rim to make a harp with a different shape.

"You gotta squeeze the water out of the wet paper," He continued. "This part takes hours. I just sit and squeeze, like I do with the beads, only it takes much longer. I also make sure that the paper is evenly distributed around the rim. I put pen inserts in place to make the necessary holes; it's best to have the paper dry with the holes already in it. It takes a couple of days to dry and paint. Then you've got your harp."

I couldn't imagine the value of one of these instruments. I had heard that a piece of his hair could fetch $100, a crude drawing, $500 if it was autographed. Geraldo Rivera did an interview with Charlie and later sold the one hour videos for $19.99. Charlie was certain that the reporter made millions of dollars from this venture.

"If you have money, you have power," Manson had ranted. "Power is strength and money will get you a lot of respect, too!" His ability to manipulate the simplest of pieces of paper and food into world-class works of art earned him my total respect, regardless of how much money he had.

From Charlie, I learned how to multi-task and get several things done at the same time. He helped motivate me to accomplish many tasks, and to aspire to great things. His ability with beads and dolls and harps encouraged me to think big and do the best that I could at everything. I may never write the songs he has or master an instrument like him, but I can still be the best that I can be.

I certainly don't want to be "brain dead" like many people in the world. Charlie often warned me about this. "Most people are not using their brains," he told me." They are just walking around like damn robots with no fucking direction whatsoever." Charlie was always moving, always creating, always thinking. I learned to do the same.

Nothing made Charlie happier while doing his time than talking about his guitar. "I sure wish I had my guitar right now," Charlie would exclaim. "I could play all day and all night. With my guitar, I go into my music and go places, man. I can make sounds that will make you wonder how I could do the sounds on a musical instrument!"

"Charlie," I replied. "I could just imagine you playing a guitar, especially an electric guitar with all of the years of experience that you have. I bet you could make some really great sounds."

"Man, I can play better than anyone you've ever heard play," boasted Charlie.

I believed him, too.

Chapter 13
Stories out of San Quentin

"The reason for evil in the world is that people are not able to tell their stories."
C.G. Jung

Charlie reminisced often about his time in San Quentin State Prison. He spent several years there, first on death row for the 7 murders in the Tate and La Bianca attacks, and then in a unit segregated from the general population when the death penalty was rescinded in California in 1972. To me, he never criticized the institution any more than any other prison in which he had served. He recounted numerous stories about events in that facility that stands in the shadow of the Golden Gate Bridge. Each story was as fascinating as the story teller.

Located in Marin County, just outside San Rafael in Northern California, San Quentin State Prison opened in 1852, making it the oldest penal institution in the state. The first prison at that location comprised a wooden ship moored in the San Francisco Bay in 1851. It was prepared to house thirty inmates. The boat prison was later replaced with a structure constructed just yards from where the boat was moored. Until 1932, the facility held women as well as men. It boasts of being the site of the first Alcoholics Anonymous meeting in 1941.

Today, it's the sole location of California's death row, housing all

146

of the state's prisoners who have been sentenced to die. Since 1996, executions have been carried out by lethal injection. Still, San Quentin retains its gas chamber. The property is so large (432 acres), and houses so many inmates (over 5,000, nearly twice its capacity) that it possesses its own postal code. Few other penal institutions in the United States have so many inmates.

Famous residents at San Quentin include Richard Ramirez, the night stalker; Scott Peterson who killed his wife and unborn son, placing them in the San Francisco Bay; and David Carpenter, the trailside killer. Nevertheless, the biggest celebrity to ever be housed in San Quentin would have to be my friend, Charles Manson.

One afternoon, while I was in my cell minding my own business, reading some books sent to me by a publishing house in San Francisco, I heard a rap on the wall. It was Charlie. "Boxcar!"

"Yeah, what's up, Charlie?" I queried.

"Back when I was in San Quentin," he said launching into a story, "some guys tried to punk me."

"Is that right, Charlie?" I was interested in what he was about to say.

"Yeah," he continued. "They said I snitched on some of my people, and told me not to come out of my cell or they'd kill me."

"Is that right, Charlie?" I repeated.

"Yeah, so I came out of my cell the first chance I could, and two big white guys are standing over me." His voice betrayed no fear. "They began yelling at me, 'we told you to not come out of your cell, you rat.'"

As Charlie spoke, he seemed to be reliving the experience. He told me how he responded to the threat: "I'm a man. Who are you to tell me not to come out of my cell? Are you a guard?"

Apparently, two other San Quentin inmates, also large men, who were friendly to Charlie, had heard the commotion. Charlie told me that they interrupted the two men who had confronted him. Charlie's friends demanded proof that Charlie had snitched.

"I never snitched on them. I ain't never finked on nobody about nothing," Charlie recounted what he had said to his attackers. Because the men could not get their stories straight to the satisfaction of Charlie's friends, the men who accused Charlie ended up wandering away like dogs with their tales between their legs. Manson impressed upon me how close he had come to being killed in that altercation.

It was evident to me that Charlie had every right to retaliate for what had been done to him by those false accusers. He could have initiated an attack on the two men, and done it with all the justification inmates gave to one another for revenge. He could've killed them or had them killed. Instead, he chose not to pursue it. He told me that he just let it go. That was Charlie: live and let live! The two accusers never bothered him again, he told me, and he never bothered them.

Later that day, Charlie continued to tell me about San Quentin. After the third watch shift changed, Charlie banged on my wall again. "Boxcar!"

"Yeah, what's up Charlie?" I inquired.

"Are you busy?" Charlie returned a question for my question.

"No, what's up, Charlie?" I asked again.

"When I was in San Quentin, there was this little bird that used to fly around the building." Why Charlie was telling me this, I didn't know. "I started to feed it, and it became so friendly to me that after a while it no longer looked anywhere else for food. It just came to me when it was hungry."

"Is that right?" I replied as I pondered why he was sharing this with me. Was he trying to tell me that I was the little bird because he looked out for me at Canteen every month? We both knew that I had no money and that he always made sure I was able to purchase something. Perhaps this was just a story that he felt the need to share. He liked to tell stories. There was no doubt about that. Sometimes, however, he liked to slip in double meanings, or talk about something through the use of stories. I enjoyed his stories, even though I was often suspicious of his intent.

On another occasion, about the same time, he told me another story about his time at San Quentin. Apparently, there was an old man in his cell block who had been wakened repeatedly by his neighbor. The neighbor spoke loudly, late into the night, night after night. Finally, Charlie told me, the old man broke down and confronted the younger man:

"'Hey, Jerry,' called out the older man.

"'What's up, Billy?' replied the younger man.

"'I'm trying to sleep at night and you are making noise when you should be quite and respectful. You might as well kill me, because if you don't then I will kill you.' The old man was not joking. 'So I'm asking you to stop that noise.'"

That was the end of Charlie's story. I knew he just wanted to talk, but I suspect he also wanted to instruct me to always stand up for myself and never show fear. After a short period of quiet, my neighbor launched into another story from his days at San Quentin. His former home seemed heavy on his mind.

"I was up on north block, Six Tier in San Quentin," he started. "There was a yard for death row inmates up on the roof. There was a big white inmate who turned toward me and asked me, 'do you have a problem with me, or do you have any plans to kill me?'"

Charlie told me that he looked at him and replied, "No, I don't have no problems with you. Do you got problems with me?"

Charlie recounted that the big inmate ambled over to him and continued, "'No, I don't have no problems with you. It's just that every time someone has come up here on this yard with me, they've come up here to start problems with me. I figured you was one of them too!'

"No, it's cool man. I don't want no problems." Charlie repeated himself to put the man at ease. He later found out that this inmate was known to attack every inmate who spent time with him in the yard. He had nearly killed a couple of men in that area who had had problems with him.

Charlie on another occasion explained to me that he alone was responsible for inmates having guitars behind bars. When he was on death's row in San Quentin, it was announced that the death penalty had been eliminated. The year was 1972. He and other death row inmates were told to prepare to be moved to cells reserved for long-term prisoners, since death row would be closed for remodeling. In addition, the inmates were asked what they wanted to possess in their new cells. Charlie had only one request: a guitar.

At the time, Charlie told me, guitars were outlawed for all inmates. The icon with a new lease on life put up such a fuss over not being allowed to stow and use a guitar that the warden ultimately caved to his request. Charlie boasted to me that all inmates were allowed to keep musical instruments in their cells because of his lobbying efforts.

Even though the death penalty has since been reinstated in California, all inmates, even those on death row, are entitled to a guitar if they want one, thanks to Charlie. A lot of inmates just think that they got it coming because they asked for it. However, if it weren't for Charlie speaking up about it, there would be no guitars or other musical instruments allowed. As it is, convicts may possess keyboards, harmonicas, congas, bongos, drum sets, and various types of stringed instruments. Later, prisons added music rooms for inmates to practice, and stages, built so that inmates could perform in talent shows and holiday festivities. All of this was made possible by the hard work and determination of Charles Manson.

Charlie and I conversed regularly after dark. It seemed like a peaceful time to chat, both of us being night owls. Charlie and I maintained very unusual sleeping patterns at times. If we chose to, we could stay up to all hours of the night and sleep for much of the day. We chose to do this often when we got into an interesting conversation in the evening. We were usually careful to be respectful of the other inmates when we talked until four or five o'clock in the morning. Inevitably, though, one of us would say that while we were enjoying our talk, we were too sleepy to keep our eyes open any longer.

Sometimes, Charlie would make a disturbance in the middle of the night. I never did. I even tried to quiet him down to respect the others a few times. No one ever told Charlie what to do, I found out. When he wants to, Charlie will make noise. Even singing or playing the bongos on his sink was not out of the question for him. The hour of the day or night seemed irrelevant to him.

Sometimes, I would initiate our conversations; other times, he got my attention first. When I was the initiator, I would call to Charlie by banging on his door or wall to call him. He would pound on the wall with his fist or tap the window with his gold ring to return my greeting. Charlie often said, "Same old; same old," when I asked him how he was doing.

A few times, our conversations transformed into a session of toasting all the important people and events in our lives. One of us would invite the other to get a shot, a small cup of coffee, pruno, or some other drink. We would bang on the walls once again, this time to signify that we had completed the task and were ready to toast.

One of us would say, "A toast to the animals." We would then take a sip of our respective beverages.

The other would add, "A toast to the brother." We would continue our toasts, back and forth, sometimes for hours, raising the name of anyone we could think to honor. We'd go through our lists of family members and friends. We'd toast fellow inmates who had done us a favor. We'd even toast famous celebrities. Everyone who deserved it received a toast from Boxcar and Charlie.

One night Charlie told me about "Squeaky," born Lynette Alice Fromme, the Manson family member who was convicted of an assassination attempt on President Gerald Ford. Squeaky had obtained a handgun and approached the thirty-eighth President of the United States while he was making a campaign stop in California. She never injured him, never even pulled the trigger, but was quickly arrested and convicted of attempted murder, a federal offense since the intended victim was the President. Charlie recounted these events for me around the thirty-fifth anniversary of the Tate murders. He added that "Red," the name he used to refer to Fromme because of her red hair and her adoration of the California Redwoods, had been eligible for parole hearings repeatedly since 1985. She'd always inquire as to whether Charlie had been paroled, according to Charlie. Since he had not, she declined to even go to her parole hearings and remained in jail. Charlie called her his "main girl," for her faithfulness.

Manson and Fromme had served a combined total of more than seventy years in prison at the time that he shared this with me. Fromme remained in a Texas federal prison, though she was eventually paroled in August of 2009. I'm sure we toasted "Red," at one of our toasting events.

Charlie educated me about so-called "professionals" during one of our many conversations. He told me that he was never impressed by anybody's status, no matter what the level of education or the job title. I observed this for myself when professional people came through the tier. He explained to me how it all worked, and why he acted the way he did. His distain for experts was most obvious when he interacted with a psych tech or a psychiatrist.

Every morning, a psych tech (short for psychiatric technician) came through our building after breakfast. Acting as some sort of an assistant psychiatrist, he announced, "Psych Tech!" loudly as he did his rounds. If anyone had a problem with sleeping, eating, feeling suicidal, or feeling depressed, the psych tech would talk to him and decide whether he needed to be referred to the psychiatric ward or whether he needed to be evaluated for medication. He would ask inmates how they were feeling, how they were sleeping, shitting, or eating. He would ask whether they felt like killing themselves or hurting other people. Charlie usually ignored these pseudo-professionals.

Once a month, the psychiatrist himself made the rounds to check on everyone who was taking medication or who was at risk. One day, our psychiatrist appeared at Charlie's cell. "Hello, Mr. Manson. I'm Doctor Lowry," the man said politely.

"Hello, Mr. Lowry. I'm Doctor Manson!" Charlie replied very loudly in an attempt to turn the tables. I couldn't help but laugh. All these workers, medical technical assistants (MTAs), psych techs, doctors, and psychiatrists, have the duty to care for the individuals in the prison, but Charlie didn't see it that way. It was apparent to him that their motives and abilities were suspect. Some professionals were uncaring, not really qualified to be care-givers on an emotional level; others lacked the skills to provide any help at all. Charlie heralded that incompetence and the apathy with that single smart remark.

He explained to me that most educated people are just play acting. Doctors, he pointed out, had to go to school and get a diploma. Once they have received this framed piece of paper, they have the right to "play" at being a doctor. If you played the role well, you made lots of money. He assured me that if someone was a good enough actor, he or she never had to get the diploma or do the schooling. A talented thespian could simply play the role, fool others, and be successful at whatever he or she wanted to do. Charlie held distain for other professionals as well, such as lawyers, judges, teachers, and the group he despised the most, namely the religious leader, whether priest, minister, or anyone who went by a title indicating a leadership role in a church. It was all a game, he explained to me. In his opinion, everybody was just being phony.

I put Charlie's words to the test one day as I attempted to outsmart the system. I told Charlie that I was going to act crazy and see how many people I could convince. He encouraged me in my plan. I wasn't exactly going to do the work of a white-collar professional, but if I could convince the administration that I was having a psychotic episode, who knows what other role I could play in this world, I reasoned.

On a subsequent night, after consuming a large quantity of pruno, my prison wine, I told "Black Bird," the inmate in the cell on the other side of me, "I want to do a cell extraction."

I wanted to see if I could convince the guards to mace me and use force to take me out of my cell. Yelling to the guards, I threatened to kill myself. I tried to act as bizarre as I could. Taking a page from Charlie's playbook, I put together all manner of nonsense phrases. The guard who responded to my disturbance asked me questions which I didn't answer. Appearing lost in my own thoughts, and oblivious to the guard's presence, I proceeded to act as though I was going to do harm to myself.

My charade worked better than I expected. I watched as 5 armed guards assembled outside my cell. When I would not cooperate, they doused my face and chest with mace from a large spray canister. The liquid attacked every moist membrane that it contacted, just as it was designed to do. It caused tears, swelling, and the sensation that my face had been splashed with 10 gallons of gasoline and sufficient flames to ignite it. It burned my nostrils, my lungs, and even my skin where there was an open sore. Once sprayed, I could think of nothing but wiping the offending liquid off my face and body. I was ready to gouge out my eyeballs and scrap my skin entirely off my face if necessary. I wondered whether I had made a good decision to fake an episode with the guards. All thoughts of resistance faded away as my attention turned toward the nearest available water. I could hear nothing except the screams that came from my eyes, nose and mouth. I may have been screaming myself.

I was soon extracted from the cell and herded to the psych ward for evaluation. It didn't take the 5 guards, dressed for war, to move me. One petit nurse could have mastered me. When I arrived at the psych ward, my acting was so convincing that I was given some kind of psychiatric medication and placed in a new cell. After about a week of boredom and talking to doctors and nurses, I was returned to my cell beside Charlie. I nearly split my stomach open with laughter when Black Bird copied me the very next day. He was gone for three days before he was returned. We got plenty of enjoyment pulling off our stunts and creating more work and stress for the guards. We talked about our exploits for hours.

Charlie was glad to see me return to my cell next to him, but he was also worried. He asked me question after question about my time in the psych ward. He was apparently afraid that I had used my cell extraction as a ruse to be taken off the tier so that I could rat against him or one of his friends. Once he realized that I'd told him the truth and once he realized that I hadn't testified against him or anyone else, he relaxed. We both knew that there are prisoners who will participate in that type of scheme in order to cooperate with the police. Secretive behavior such as that is often discovered and the snitch is appropriately dealt with by the other inmates.

As I had expected, Charlie had asked lots of questions in my absence, confirming the information upon my return. He was always cautious with others; he had good reason to be paranoid.

As far as the guards were concerned, I had had a real episode of "crazy." I have the paperwork to prove how fooled they were. I should've received an Academy Award for my acting. Now, I have the belief that if I set my mind to it, I could play act as a doctor, priest, or even lawyer!

Charlie showed great pleasure to see me return, especially after he concluded that I had, in fact, remained loyal to him. Guards on the unit told me that Charlie wanted me back. My friend had requested that the cell be retained for me—and it was—for eight days! Usually, a void is filled within twenty-four hours when an inmate it taken to the psych ward, often with a newbie from the next incoming bus.

I refrained from exhibiting crazy behavior once I proved to myself that I could con the guards. I didn't want to take any more medication I didn't need, and I wearied of the extra attention I received from the prison psychologists. It pleased Charlie that I stopped acting crazy. It had upset him that I was doing so much to torment the guards. He was afraid for the added attention that my behavior would bring. I listened to him when he suggested that I start acting sensible. I think I was growing up, thanks in no small part to him. I began to utilize my time with more reading and drawing, instead of fighting against the system.

Charlie's many television interviews included more than a bit of acting on his part. He explained that he was frequently playing to the cameras. If he were to give straight answers, or dull statements without any unusual antics, the piece might not have made it on the air, despite his notoriety. He informed me that he was acutely aware of his audience when he spoke--whenever he spoke. During the Geraldo interview, for instance, he was directing the action. He told the cameramen where to position the cameras and what shots to use.

"Geraldo and the camera crew were afraid of me," he laughed. "They did what I told them to do because they knew that I am an expert on how to put on a show."

Charlie confided in me that much of what he did for the cameras was play acting. When Diane Sawyer interviewed him, he made sure to put on a fearsome, evil demeanor. "That kind of show," he explained, "sells tickets and brings in viewers." He really didn't care what others thought of him, as long as they were entertained and continued tune into him.

It bothered him that Geraldo was portrayed as a tough guy. "I was far tougher than Geraldo," Charlie bragged. "It wasn't until I was in handcuffs that Geraldo started to do his 'macho' thing," It also bothered him that Geraldo sold millions of dollars worth of the video, while he made no money at all.

In addition to his interest in music and his desire to play act, Charlie wanted to change the current state of prison life. He admitted that he himself was securely protected and relatively affluent behind bars. "My situation is not typical," he told me. "Most inmates don't have the money that I have. They have nothing and no one to take care of them."

Charlie helped me understand that the whole prison system is in dire need of change. Little by little, through our conversations, he showed me that there were problems, and suggested possible actions to improve the system. For nearly thirty years, inmates have had their rights violated by the extensive and indiscriminate financial cuts to prison programs. Almost every area of inmate life has been affected by rationings in the funding for prisons and prisoners. The lack of educational opportunities among inmates as a result of eliminated vocational training, and prison over-crowding, for examples, make the current situation only a faint shadow of what prisons once were.

There was a time when prisons were devoted to the rehabilitation of inmates, Charlie related to me. Since most inmates would be back on the streets again someday, great effort was done to educate, train, and build up the self-esteem of prisoners. That was the best way to fight the high rates of recidivism and the increase in crime. Accordingly, prisons aided their residents in obtaining degrees, finding vocations, and learning to love themselves and others. Classes were encouraged, even mandated for some prisoners. Professors were brought in from nearby colleges. Each prisoner was put on a long-term guidance plan.

Governor Pete Wilson, and his political cronies, began deep budget cuts from which the system has never recovered, despite the fact that his administration was followed by numerous other governors and legislatures. Today, as a result of financial corner-cutting, most programs have either been eliminated or severely scaled back. Even the quality of food provided to prisoners has suffered. Refined sugar has been replaced by artificial sweeteners that are known to be cancer-causing agents. Second-rate food is now regularly passed off as a meal simply because it has sufficient calories and nutritional content.

The medical needs of inmates have also been overlooked. Charlie didn't need to tell me about this. I witnessed first hand that inmates who break an ankle are provided with medical technical assistants (MTAs), and not doctors and nurses. They are provided with ice for the swelling, rather than the needed X-rays. Medications are also withheld from all but the most severe cases, as if the system can save a few pennies by stingily hoarding what is needed by the inmates. People need to realize that when prisoners are denied proper dental and medical care, the whole of society suffers.

The flawed system relies too much on the grievance process. Authorities won't take action unless, and until, a 602 grievance form is filled out and submitted, if even then. The grievance process can take up to six months or longer. It would be in the prison's best interest, and in the interest of the inmate, to initiate a preventative and pre-emptive system that anticipates the inmate's needs and works to meet them. As it is, the system is unsympathetic until a crisis happens. Then, once a form is filled out, it may take months before any action is taken. By this time, much of the damage is beyond repair.

Most inmates, nearly 90 percent of them, are in prison on a drug and alcohol related charges, or were found to be under the influence of drugs and alcohol when they committed the acts for which they are incarcerated. Clearly, the system needs to deal effectively with these chemical intoxicants before any productive reforms can be implemented. Prosecutors and judges need to make the temporary insanity defense more readily available to defendants: if alcohol and certain drugs are legal, then we can't hold it against individuals who make one or two bad choices while under the influence. Preventative efforts would pay valuable dividends here, too.

Charlie was very much into the community idea of care. When we spoke about the needs of inmates, we meant all the needs of the entire population. We didn't single out the rich or white collar criminal, the one who seems to receive preferential treatment today. Charlie told me that a society is only as good as its care for its lowest members. It was the lowest that he cared for when he was out of prison; it was the lowest for which he provided when he expressed his generosity behind bars.

To emphasize his point, Charlie repeated a story that he had already told me. Whether it was from forgetfulness (maybe Alzheimer's) or from a need to reinforce what he had previously said, I don't know. He related to me again that while he was in San Quentin, he befriended a bird. The small sparrow grew to trust and rely on him. "The bird started to get so used to me feeding it," he said, "that it no longer went to find its own food. It just came to me."

Chapter 14
Charlie's Health

"It is health that is real wealth and not pieces of gold and silver."
Mohandas Gandhi

Charles Manson was transferred to the California Medical Facility (CMF) from San Quentin in 1974. Located in Vacaville, CMF is a prison hospital in Northern California that treats all the inmates who are mentally ill, crippled, intellectually challenged, and whoever else wants to go there for whatever reason or ailment. It was built in 1955, and now stands next to the Northern California Prison, a reception center for the inmates who come fresh from the streets or from a county jail to be processed for prison. In addition to psych-evaluations, CMF conducts educational aptitude tests and other evaluations to see whether convicts can be placed in a job. Classification scores are aggregated to determine where inmates would be best suited within the system.

Charlie told me: "They sent me to Vacaville to have a psych evaluation and they started pumping me with all kinds of psycho-tropic drugs. It was done involuntarily and I was taking medication I didn't need. They just kept giving me pill after pill!"

Charlie complained of many ailments, but he wasn't interested in taking any medication. In fact, he refused to take pills offered to him by the institution. He feared being poisoned, I guessed. To this day, I'm not sure how many of his supposed maladies were real and how many were imagined. He talked about some of his disorders, only hinting at others. Inmates sometimes confirmed his disorders to me, but I don't know whether they got their information from him or from some other source. I knew that Charlie didn't spend any time in the infirmary.

He once told me that he had cancer and was nearing the end of his life. Possibly, this was another of his oblique or indirect references to death which didn't necessarily correlate to reality. Nevertheless, he often spoke of his cancer in ways that sounded convincing. He would never tell me where in his body it started, saying that it didn't matter. He informed me that it had spread to his lungs and his stomach, possibly his colon as well. He told me that he was able to remain strong, despite the cancer, only because he could control his strength with his mind. He was stronger than his cancer and would eventually rid his whole body of it, he bragged to me.

He also spoke of other health challenges: emphysema from a lifetime of chain smoking, facial burns from a prison attack in Vacaville in 1984, stomach problems from a Drano poisoning he endured at San Quentin, miscellaneous heart troubles, and depression born of the hopelessness of his lengthy incarceration. I always suspected that he had the added burden of the early stages of senility, but I was never certain of this.

There was another reason that Charlie was moved from San Quentin to Vacaville, I learned. He was having gang problems at his former home. There had been some threats made to him by the Mexican Mafia which was powerful in San Quentin. Had he remained where he was, someone eventually would have gotten to him and cut short his life. At Vacaville, Charlie was free from those threats because that prison was controlled by a gang that was an enemy of the Mexican Mafia. It gets complicated at times to follow the different gangs and their battles with each other, but in this case, the enemy of Charlie's enemy became his friend and savior in his new institution. While Charlie never joined any gangs (indeed, he was a one-man gang), he did make some affiliations that helped protect him. These associations could rile up other antipathetic gangs and precipitate the breathing of violent threats.

Charlie suggested to me that his excuse of going to the CMF in

Vacaville was just a cover, a reason to spiriting him away from the threats. I am not sure whether this is true or not. It is possible that Charlie didn't want to appear mentally ill to me. Some inmates will come up with all sorts of excuses about why they go to CMF or why they had a psych-evaluation done--excuses that carefully veil the truth that they suffered from one form of mental illness or another.

In light of his physical ailments, there were times I wondered whether Charlie would die while being housed right next to me. I had lived on tiers long enough to know what it's like when another inmate passes away. If a fight is not involved, usually the event happens quietly, often during sleep. I have been incarcerated in several places where the morning shift found a body and had to transport it to the prison morgue. Death makes you feel uncomfortable, but you get used to it. It's a fact of life. Among the circles within which I associate, it's the only way most inmates find their release from prison.

It was possible, I sometimes thought, that I would be the last person to which this famous icon would speak, granting me the privilege of hearing this man's final words. I assured myself that if he were to die in his sleep some night, I would be able to recall our conversations from the previous night, including the final sentence or two before we said our "good nights." I was sure that the media would want to know his last utterances.

When I asked Charlie about his time at the California Medical Facility, he said, "They gave me a job in the chapel. The door to the chapel was locked. The preacher opened the door, and closed and locked it behind me. As I looked around, I saw a real mess. There was a tall Indian about seven feet in height who was breaking out little squares from the stained glass window. They were setting me up with this Indian so that something might happen to me while he was in a rage. Fortunately, we became friends and cleaned up the mess together.

"Eventually," Charlie continued, "we striped the old wax off the floor and polished it. We repaired the windows he had damaged. The room became as clean and shiny as a hallway at McNeal Island."

He told me that they also planted a garden along side of the building with fruit and vegetables. Another Native American suggested that they create a sweat lodge, which they built to provide his group with a place to gather.

Charlie shared with me many stories in which he straightened out a mess in the prison. In his words, he was always the hero, always the one who solved the problem or created the solution. Not only at CMF, it appeared to me that Charlie was the champion of every institution he ever visited.

He once related to me, "There were some inmates in the psych unit making a lot of noise, banging on the doors, breaking the windows, and flooding the tiers. They clogged the toilets and sinks, while running the water, until the tier was flowing with ankle-deep water. There was trash everywhere.

"I went and got a bucket of hot water." Charlie continued. "I showed it to each one of the trouble makers. I threatened to throw it in their faces unless they stopped what they were doing."

Charlie was almost giddy as he narrated these events. "When some of them thought I was bluffing. I had to use one of them as an example. I grabbed him by the hair and smashed his face into a door. I cleaned up the mess after they stopped and never had any trouble on that unit again."

Charlie must have wanted to talk. He moved on to a new story to share other events at CMF as I listened intently to his tales. "I was always in my cell prior to getting a job in the chapel," Charlie explained to me. "One day Babo Sosa, the leader of the Nuestra Familia, and two members of his gang opened my cell with a screw driver. I thought they were going to kill me. They explained that I would be safe with them because they had no problems with me."

Despite his position as the leader of the notorious gang, Babo Sosa was replaced, Charlie told me. When his effectiveness waned, a younger leader was raised to take his place in the early 1990s. For Sosa, this was no 401K retirement plan. When you leave this type of an organization, you usually do so in a casket. He was only able to survive by the protection of some of his loyal members. His health caught up to him, however, during a prison transfer when he suddenly died. While his death certificate declares the cause of his demise to be a heart attack, many aren't convinced that he died naturally.

Charlie then told me about a deadly situation in CMF that could easily have ended his life. He began: "Hey Boxcar. In Vacaville, there was a chair I used to sit in on the tier. It was red. This new kid came into the unit from the hole. The whites found out he wanted to be part of their crew, and wanted to really earn his bones. They sent him to kill me. I sensed that this kid had some fear in him, and really didn't realize what he was getting into, or exactly who he was sent to kill.

"I seen he had a knife in his pocket," Charlie bragged, "and I asked him to show me the knife. He showed it to me, and I told him to give it to me, and to explain to me why he had it. He told me he was sent to kill me in order to be a part of the Arian Brotherhood, an ally of the Mexican Familia. Well, this kid was as harmless as a butterfly. After handing me the knife, and telling me what I already knew, he was deemed 'no good' by those who had sent him. He couldn't go back to be with them in the hole or be a part of their gang!"

A few days later, I saw an inmate spit on Charlie's window when Charlie was only a few inches from it. I could feel the pain in Charlie as he dealt with it. I could tell that it hurt him, even though Charlie knew how to deal with it from his years of incarceration. The guilty party, not a friend of anyone in the tier, had shouted after he spat. "You're a piece of shit, Charles Manson. You're a baby killer. Rot in hell you son of a bitch." The outburst may have been a reaction to the clan outfit that Charlie had worn on the tier. More likely, the man was crazy or he was bitter over Charlie's notoriety. Perhaps both.

Charlie yelled back at the guy at the top of his lungs. "You can't hurt me! You haven't done anything to me that hasn't already been done to me. I'm not P.C. They got me locked behind this door to protect YOU. They put me in P.C., not P.C. in me. I'm Charles Manson, a serial killer, death row, dead man walking three times. I'm already dead. You can't kill me or hurt me. I am no one. I'm lower than a bug. I've been doing this since I was a juvenile.

"You mess with my water, my air, my food, my clothes, my blankets, my sheets, my socks, my boxers, my mail, my visits," Charlie continued. "You tell my visitors not to visit me. You steal my mail, steal my music, tell me I can't draw pictures." By this time, it appeared that he was yelling at the whole prison system, perhaps venting a diffuse rage at all mankind.

"The Justice Department has told me that I can't have money because its 'illegal business practice,'" Charlie went on. "I got people lying on me: they send the Secret Service to talk to me and say I asked them to help me kill the United States President. I ain't said none of that. They just want a get-out-of-jail-free card. Your spit don't bother me. So what you gonna do now?"

The tier got quiet, as it often did after a Charles Manson outburst. If the inmate who spat took issue with anything Charlie said, he didn't vocalize it.

Sometimes, Charlie would put on what I called his, "mad man mask." He would scream at the top of his lungs. He would do this even for visitors who could only see him, and not hear what he was saying. To this sound, he would add the visuals of someone shooting a pistol in the most menacing fashion. He would yell, "Bang, bang, bang," while pulling the imagined triggers, as though he were holding real six-shooters. I sometimes wondered how much fear he put into those prison visitors who came by just for a look.

Most inmates were good at tuning Charlie out during one of his rages. We would listen to the first few lines, and then busy ourselves with reading, writing, watching television, or whatever we were working on. I often put earplugs in my ears to filter out his voice. It was understood that we all have blow ups from time to time. After a while, Charlie would cool down and life would go on.

It didn't bother Charlie to disturb others with loud noises, sometimes even in the middle of the night. Why others didn't object to this act of disrespect, I never understood. I suspect it was because of his notoriety. Maybe, they feared there would be retribution if they objected to Charlie's obnoxious behaviors. I just ignored him as I ignored other inmates who were disrespectful. I have found that objecting usually doesn't help. I wait for other, more menacing inmates, to keep disruptive people in line. My days of being the enforcer of a tier are long gone. I don't want the conflict or the attention I craved in my earlier days. I suppose Charlie is responsible for helping mellow out my behavior. Ironically, he more than anyone else benefited from my new passive attitude.

One night, I was wakened at about two o'clock in the morning. I heard the drum beat of someone playing his sink like a set of bongos. At first, I couldn't determine from where the sound was emanating. Eventually, I recognized the voice that was singing along, and was able to locate its source. It was Charlie. He was chanting while playing bongos on his steel sink. He showed some talent, too. I would love to have heard him pound out a beat on a real set, just not at two in the morning.

He played slowly, then fast. He was able to vary his beat across two distinct sounds: low, low, low; high, high, high. It would sound terrific as part of some group of musicians, I thought. Eventually, Charlie drifted off into the silence of sleep and allowed me to resume my slumber.

Charlie was not always noisy. When he was depressed, he could get really quiet. I would become so concerned sometimes that I would check on him from time to time, just to make sure that he was okay. When he thought about being denied visits from children, or the freedom he once enjoyed to pass out gloves to the tower guards, he would become melancholy. Sometimes, he would make self-destructive threats:

"I should just hang myself," Charlie said somberly to me one day, "so I don't have to deal with all this mess about my visits, mail, or being able to roam in the prison. I used to walk around passing out the latex gloves to all the units on 4-A yard. I planted flowers and grass, and now they spray me with mace, take my tennis shoes, jeans, food and tell me I can't write my music or paint or play my guitar!"

I knew that Charlie was too mentally strong to actually kill himself. After all that he had been through with his difficult upbringing and his run-ins with the law, I knew he would be brave and face his difficulties like a man, like the true inmate he was, one who knew how to handle his responsibilities. Still, I worried. I would call to Charlie from my cell on regular intervals to ensure his safety. I wanted to be able to notify the guards if he did in fact attempt harm to himself. Each time I went to yard or shower, I would glance at him through his window to ensure he was in good shape. Eventually, he would get over his melancholia. He always did. Usually, it ended with a request for a talk.

"Boxcar," Charlie would say quietly. "Are you busy?" We would then launch into a long discussion that told me that Charlie was himself once again.

Chapter 15
Charlie's Future

"Do not dwell in the past, do not dream of the future,
concentrate the mind on the present moment."
The Buddha

Some people love Charles Manson; many more hate him. Some are drawn to him because of a fascination with the horror of his crimes. Others detest him and are glad that he was tried and convicted for those exact same crimes. There are also those who want nothing more than to kill him. How many nobodies have achieved infamy by killing or attempting to kill some well-known celebrity? Everyone, including Charlie himself, knows that the name of the person who ends Charles Manson's life will go down in history and be forever linked with his. Many who cannot achieve attention from him, and who have no life of which to be proud, would love to kill him and thus be immortalized. If it were not for the murders of certain famous people, we'd never have learned the names of Mark Chapman, Lee Harvey Oswald, or John Wilkes Booth. Charlie lives with the knowledge that his death could be the ticket to someone else's fame.

I came to love Charlie because of who he is as a person. Personally, I do not like people who hurt women and children. I especially despise those who harm people who are the most unable to defend themselves, such as the elderly and the disabled. If Charlie were guilty of such crimes toward the weak, I wouldn't want to associate with him. There have been many child killers and those who preyed upon the elderly that I have refused to befriend. In my opinion, Charlie did not harm those in need, regardless of any jury verdict. He helped the weak.

I wasn't attracted to Charlie because of his fame. High visibility draws its share of stalkers, whether the celebrity is an actor, sports figure, or politician, but I am nobody's follower. It wasn't the crimes that held any attraction to me either, the kind of attraction that draws others to a fascination with the lives of serial killers like Jeffrey Dahmer, John Wayne Gacy, or Ted Bundy. My decision to associate with Charles Manson was made only to give the man the benefit of the doubt. As I held off on my judgments of him, I began to see an interesting and very complex individual, one who is talented yet horribly wronged by society, one who therefore is capable of much good and much bad.

Charlie repeatedly told me that he was innocent of the wrongs for which he was convicted. Now, I am no fool. I would have to be completely gullible to believe a prisoner at his word. I know that most inmates proclaim their innocence. I did. Even in the face of overwhelming evidence, much of it found on my person at the time of my arrest, I claimed that I had been wrongly arrested and falsely convicted. I was found guilty of fourteen felonies in the aftermath of two separate crime sprees, including grand theft and attempted murder. There is now no need to uphold the charade of my innocence. I am not proud of what I have done, but I am prepared to take responsibility for my actions. With all my appeals expended, there is not much point in denying the obviousness of my guilt. Charlie's case is another matter, however.

I gave Charlie a chance. It's not that I accepted his plea of innocence. I didn't, at least not at first. It has been said that if you released all the prisoners who proclaimed their innocence, there would be no one left to guard. This statement is probably true. Most inmates who have spoken with me about their crimes either minimize their crimes or deny any guilt. I suspected that the old man was doing that with me also. Still, I wanted to know him for who he was, and not for what had been written about him throughout the years. I had heard the stories and listened to news reports. Since I know that today's media will report something (or hold something back) irrespective of its truth, and since I know that our justice system wrongly claims that someone is innocent until proven guilty, I decided to get to know the man and form my own opinions.

From what I gleaned from my conversations with the old man, I believe that Charlie was not in the Tate house when the murders were committed, and that he is innocent of those crimes, as well as the murders at the La Bianca residence. Even if he is guilty, who of us is without sin? How can we convict him, keep him in prison all his life, while we participate in the same violence through our television and through our military? Perhaps society is guiltier than Charles Manson. Maybe the system in which we all live is guilty of creating Charlie.

I considered Charlie for months, pondering who he is and what his presence beside me meant. After hours of reflection, I finally arrived at peace about Manson's identity. He is hard to classify since there is no one like him. He is a celebrity, and his notoriety has become a feedback loop. Many people have emerged who think he's great simply because of his unusual beliefs or his bizarre behavior. They are likely hoping to obtain something out their contact with Manson. Because there are so many people around him who are fascinated by him, others can't help but notice. He is a celebrity because he is a celebrity; people are interested in him because so many people are interested in him. Even with his connection to the horrendous events at two murder scenes, even with his life spent mostly in one institution or another, many attribute to him godlike characteristics, and want no more than to receive some kind of attention from him.

Regardless of his notoriety, his fans, and the players hoping to exploit him, I happened upon Charlie completely by chance. I never requested a living arrangement that left me open to his manipulations. It could be argued that I deserved it, that I had found my place in the world by my own anger and stupidity. Yet, I had to believe that there was some deeper meaning in my serendipitous path that crossed Charlie's. I have come to understand Charlie as the complex mix of a cult leader and an organized crime boss. He embodies both identities. To see him as any less is to not appreciate the force of his character.

He is a man's man, in many ways. He is the super "alpha" male in our society. If there is one thing that he desires, indeed demands, it is absolute power and control. Accordingly, he demanded an absolute allegiance of his followers back in the 1960s, far surpassing anything that David Koresh, Jim Jones, or any other well-known cult leader required of his or her minions. His demands were backed up by murderous threats and example killings that any organized crime boss would recognize. During the hippie movement, he was a religious leader and the center of a crime syndicate, all rolled into one organization and represented in one, lone human who became a cultural icon. He accomplished all he did with an almost total lack of education.

While he preached good and evil, Charlie also embodied it. Where there is good, there is evil also. This needs to be understood to have a correct perspective on Charlie. Charlie's dark sides, his infatuation with fear and death, stemmed from the fact that he believes himself to be the antichrist in the flesh. People in positions of power have to believe in their own abilities or they will not be held in great esteem by their followers. Charlie came to believe that he could control all situations that faced him and his "family." Yet deep down, Charlie always knew that he was nothing more than a disadvantaged, unwanted child who grew into a troubled adult. Charlie spent his life on a crusade to prove himself, somehow, somewhere.

Partly as a result of his troubled upbringing and his ability to manipulate, and partly due to the demands of his followers, Charlie began to display Messianic qualities. He believed himself to be Jesus Christ returned to the world. However, his low self-esteem led him to believe that his charm alone was insufficient to lead his flock. He told his family members in the 1960s that he was not only Jesus but also the Devil, in the same way that he told this to me, over and over. Now that I understand Charlie a little bit more, I can understand what he was doing.

He was controlling others in any way he could. If you hit a dog hard enough and often enough, he will become violent and bite. Unloved, abused, neglected, and abandoned, Manson came to be attracted to evil as a means to gain the upper hand over others. He identified with evil, but always claimed righteousness at the same time. He liked the German Swastika, the five pointed star, and any other sign or symbol that was embraced by Satan worshippers. Though he studied Satanism, as well as Scientology, hypnotism, and a host of other philosophies and practices, he never fully embraced any of them. He instead chose a philosophy of eclecticism that eagerly embraced evil and anything that was frightening and intimidating. Concurrently, he proclaimed the good, claiming innocence and purity for himself. It was a conflicted philosophy that accomplished exactly what Charlie desired: confusion among his followers and enemies alike. While muddling the thoughts of others, Charlie could remain firmly in control.

Charlie is the most manipulative, psychologically astute, resourceful and cunning person that I've ever met. He is able to read people and craft his message into words that will entice his audience. He has been accused of meting out mind control. This is true in as much as he is able to figure out what motivates others and use this knowledge to his own advantage. It is this cunning and manipulativeness that prompted Rolling Stone magazine to label Charlie as "the most dangerous man alive." At times, I wondered whether I had been given narcotics by him, particularly LSD, because the effect he had on me had been so great.

As I came to understand who he was and what made him tick, I feel I grew personally, and I learned not to fear him. He was nothing to be afraid of, even though he could talk tough and yell loudly. He wasn't dangerous, and may never have been. If he were ever released, he would be a curiosity, a celebrity, and an icon of the 1960s, but probably nothing more. He is all these things already. Despite his threats, breathed in bravado, I have no reason to believe that anyone would actually be killed, or any laws would be broken. Charlie would likely promote edgy products like motorcycles and mixed martial arts matches. He would live in Malibu, enjoying a large beachfront property. He would entertain guests and throw poolside parties. For a laugh, he would make threats and stir up some controversy or another. Through a careful public relations campaign, he would increase his fame and enjoy the fortune that his notoriety would bring. He would also continue to mellow as he advanced in age.

Charlie never expressed to me a desire to be set free. He told me on several occasions that he didn't want parole.

"This is my life. I don't know what it is like to be on the outside." he once said. In the past, he attended parole hearings, even requested to be released. He knew he would be denied, however. He claimed that the same government that had set him up and convicted him would be there to ensure that he was never released. He had come to accept that; in his mind, it was the price he paid for being so good to so many people. In his opinion, the world was not ready for the truth that he taught, perhaps never would be. It was not ready to face up to its own criminality, its own destruction of the environment, and its own systemic injustices.

If he were ever granted his freedom again, he once told me, he would return to Southern California. He admitted to me that he wouldn't know who to visit or where to go, specifically, but he loved the area for its beauty and its weather. He loved the Hollywood sunsets, the warm winters, and the soothing swims in the Pacific Ocean.

Epilogue

In time, I was transferred to my current prison home, Pleasant Valley State Correctional Center, exactly 180 miles from San Francisco and 180 miles from Los Angeles. Though I am only a few miles away from my former home, I might as well be on the other side of the solar system. I could not be further from Charlie if I were on another planet.

I was glad to be away from Corcoran when I left. To be moved, for me, was a dream come true. I was not happy with the prison officials at Corcoran. I didn't trust them after repeated disruptions, including changes to schedules, skipped trips to the yard, and a general feeling that no one was responsible for anything. A prisoner has very little control over his life. When schedules are changed haphazardly and promised activities are cancelled, it is really hard on an inmate's psyche. There were times that I was ready to scream because of the repeated failures and false promises of the system.

I had requested the transfer to that horrible facility in the first place, and that only made my time there more difficult: I had no one to blame but myself. I requested a transfer to yet another institution in the knowledge that no prison could be as bad as Corcoran. I was given permission to transfer away from there within weeks of my initial request. I was elated.

Yet, the joy of being transferred away was tempered by the loss of my friendship with Charlie. I had gotten to know him so well. I felt so close to him that to leave him was like having a limb removed. I had been changed by the man in such a way that I could never go back to my former self. I only wish that I could still be near him to learn and grow more. It would be nice to dream that Charlie could be transferred here someday, but I know how unlikely that is.

The first days here in Pleasant Valley were the most difficult as I adjusted to new surroundings, new guards, and no late-night conversations with "the old man." I came to know new people here, but it was not the same. I burned inside as I lay in bed reminiscing about our good times. As an inmate, observing many prison transfers, both my own and others', I have grown accustomed to saying, "Good bye," but this time it was different. It really hurt to leave Charlie. I was seared with a pain that I cannot even begin to describe. I had held off on my transfer request for many months because I enjoyed talking to Charlie so much.

I have had to do much reconsidering, these past few months. With Charlie no longer around, with no more of his stories and no more of his charming smiles, the silver in his tongue has started to tarnish. I have begun to see him in a new light. Perhaps, I needed him at the time to teach me and counsel me. Now it is time for me to move on, to rely on myself and my own abilities. I have started to notice that some of the things he taught me were not helpful or true.

He told me on repeated occasions that he was born on the same day that the United States Marine Corps was founded. That made a great story, adding to his mythic stature. If he were born at the same time as the Marine Corps, he must be strong, self reliant, and as bold as a marine. Perhaps that whole corps is strong only because of its association with Charles Manson. However, I later found out that the Marine Corps was founded near the birth of our country, in 1775. His tale was a lie so large that it defied challenge for years.

I began to wonder whether he got other facts wrong too. Did fellow inmates have a similar experience of believing Charlie at his word because he was so charming and compelling? His strength, borne out of a thousand conflicts and abusive events in his life, could intimidate anyone, could even compel someone to sidestep common reason. Maybe the facts of his stories, or some of the stories themselves, were only convenient excuses to assert control or build his reputation. Stories are a dime and dozen behind bars. One who can tell convincing stories to an inmate must be a veritable Shakespearean actor.

Many of the stories Charlie told me did prove true. I believe that he made every effort to be honest with me. He repeatedly told me to be truthful to him; it's nice to see that for the most part, he was honest as well. Other stories remain unconfirmed, however. I want to believe them, just as I want to believe the man. I will give him the benefit of the doubt until it can be proven otherwise. I guess I still owe him that level of respect. He has done so much good to me, and for me, that I cannot now join the chorus of voices that call for his obliteration. Sure, he has his bad side—who doesn't? However, it's his good side for which I plan to remember him. Perhaps, he has gained a control over me that I cannot easily shed. If that is the case, I don't care. He's such a great person who has given so much of himself that I cannot now, nor ever will be able to, hate him. I remain a Charles Manson lover, though my adoration is tinged with the reality that he may have been involved in some exceedingly heinous crimes.

Historians may not remember his good side. Future generations may only see a violent, death-obsessed cult leader. However, for good or ill, he has become an icon in our society. While he may have contributed negative elements to the 1960s, he has also become a spokesperson for a 1960s type of love and for respectful treatment of Mother Earth. He is also a role model for personal self-confidence. For better or worse, we need to acknowledge him and his notoriety. We ignore him or call him names to our own detriment. What does it say about our society that we celebrate Charles Manson? What commentary does Charlie provide to our society about how we can make it better and avoid raising additional "Charlie's" in our midst?

I hope you have enjoyed reading this book as much as I have enjoyed putting down in words what has happened to me, what I saw and heard, and how I was transformed in the process of my dealings with Charles Manson. I hope you are proud to read about a real convict and how I handled my business the way it's supposed to be handled: with loyalty, honor, respect, and love. It's my hope that his book will have a positive affect on you, even as it sheds light on a dark chapter of our past and clarifies some misconceptions and provides new information about an American celebrity.

I remain pleased with my association with Charlie. I am happy to consider myself a "family" member, even though I was not present in his heyday. I never knew the old man on the outside, but I have followed him nonetheless. I didn't participate in any of his murders, or agree to do anything wrong simply because he told me to, but I still claim him as my own. Whether he concurs or not, I wear with pride the title, "the last member of the Manson Family."

Guillermo "Boxcar" Mendez
Pleasant Valley State Prison, California, 2013

Glossary:

Ace Duce: two prisoners who watch each others' backs and offer protection on the streets or in jail, in peace and in war. Each will fight to the death, or kill, for the other.

Board-up: to cover the cell windows from the inside to prevent the "one time" or guard from seeing inside the cell. It gives the guard cause to open the door to the cell, unscheduled, at any time of day or night.

Bullet: one year in the system. For example, "I have two bullets to do and one bullet on parole."

Car: any type of weight used on the end of a string, rope or fishing line, such as a rock or piece of wood. To receive an item from an inmate in another cell, a "car" is slid or thrown to the other cell, affixed with a note or item, then pulled back by its "fish line" or string.

Care Package: a bag of items for someone who is serving time. Generally, it consists of hygiene items such as soap, razor, deodorant, toothpaste, comb, and toothbrush. It sometimes contains candy, food, cigarettes, envelopes, stamps, writing paper, and pens.

Convict: a seasoned veteran within the prison system who has done time instead of letting the time do him. He does not need a guide to instruct him on how to do time because, for him, it is a way of life.

Generally, he is a career criminal on the life plan, doing one year at a time.

Deck: a pack of cigarettes. Ten decks is a stack, or carton, of cigarettes.

Dig: "Do you understand what I am saying?" or, "are you following me?" This term was used by hippies in the late 1960s. Charles Manson continues to use this term: like most inmates, his cultural growth arrested once he entered the system.

Fish line: string, rope or fishing line used with a weight, called a "car," to transport items from one cell to another.

House: a cell. It's someone's home. Like a castle, it is to be defended at all costs. A house is out of bounds to everyone except those who have been given explicit permission to enter. Violation of another inmate's "house" merits death.

Inmate: one of a new generation of prisoners locked up in the county jail or prison. Generally he has to be told what to do in these environments by the convicts who know how to do their time. It is often used at a catch-all phrase for anyone incarcerated.

J-Cat: someone who is taking medication for a psychological disorder, such as a person who is on a mood-altering drug for mental illness, or someone who merely acts crazy.

Kite: a message, note, or letter passed from one inmate to another when direct communication isn't possible. A "kite" is passed with a fish line or hand to hand through any number of inmates.

OG: original gangster, a veteran who has been around the system a long time, at least twenty years, someone who can handle himself and those around him well. He knows how to think correctly when split second timing is required. Double OG is forty years in the system; triple OG is sixty years.

One time: a cop or guard walking or patrolling an area. Usually, he doesn't walk a beat and appears, unexpectedly, only once, and hence the name. It's also used as a warning to the inmates in the immediate area to be aware.

PC: protective custody, a status that an inmate is given by the prison when he needs extra protection from other inmates. It entails additional locks on the cell door, and a strict schedule to minimize contact with other prisoners. To Charlie, it was a badge of dishonor implying that he wasn't able to protect himself.

Pruno: prison-made wine made from fruit mash and sugar that has been fermented over a period of time, usually with artificial heat. It's contraband, but readily available behind bars. It's also called, "pulky."

Road Dog: someone you spend time with and protect. He is similar to an Ace Duce, but only in prison or jail.

Shot: a drink of coffee, Kool-Aid, or Pruno.

Shutdown: the word signifying that it is time to relax from a long day, time to go to sleep, stay off the tier, and show respect to your follow prisoners. Around ten o'clock in the evening, the first inmate desiring to sleep will yell, "shutdown," to quite down the tier.

Soul: the core of a human being, the spiritual part of man wanted by both God and the Devil. It's to be cherished and guarded. Charles Manson used "soul" as a term of endearment when addressing close confidants.

.

ACKNOWLEDGMENTS

I am thankful to "Boxcar," aka Willie Mendez, for allowing me to tell his story, a personal intimate tale of mistakes and failure, but also of redemption and hope.

I am thankful for the undying love and personal sacrifice of my wife, Linda, and my son, Forrest. Without them, this work would never have been undertaken, let alone completed.

In gratitude, I acknowledge the important part that my publisher has played in the production of this book and the copy you are holding.

Above all, to God be the glory for His love, grace, and incomparable forgiveness.

ABOUT THE AUTHORS

Mark Hewitt is a true crime author and the editor of "Radians and Inches," the scholarly, peer-reviewed journal dedicated to the search for the Zodiac serial killer. Corresponding with Charles Manson for the past ten years on a variety of personal and professional topics, Mark has become a Manson expert. Holding two Masters Degrees, he is an award-winning public speaker and world traveler. He now resides in Northern California where he researches and writes, while completing his PhD.

Willie Mendez became institutionalized as a young man after repeated violations of the law, including attempted murder and armed robbery. He is serving a 68-year prison sentence in the California penal system. His frequent outbursts landed him next to Charles Manson, the iconic 1960s serial killer. Mendez was introduced to Mark Hewitt by Manson who thought the two had similar ideas and a shared optimism for life. From his initial feelings of contempt toward the aging killer, Willie, nicknamed, "Boxcar," traveled to a place of openness and acceptance of the old man's ideas, until finally freeing himself from the control and manipulation in which he had become entangled.

Mendez is pursuing his love of art, and hopes to write a book on the many high-profile inmates and famous prison guards he has met.

CPSIA information can be obtained at www.ICGtesting.com
Printed in the USA
LVOW10s1241221214

419949LV00001B/137/P